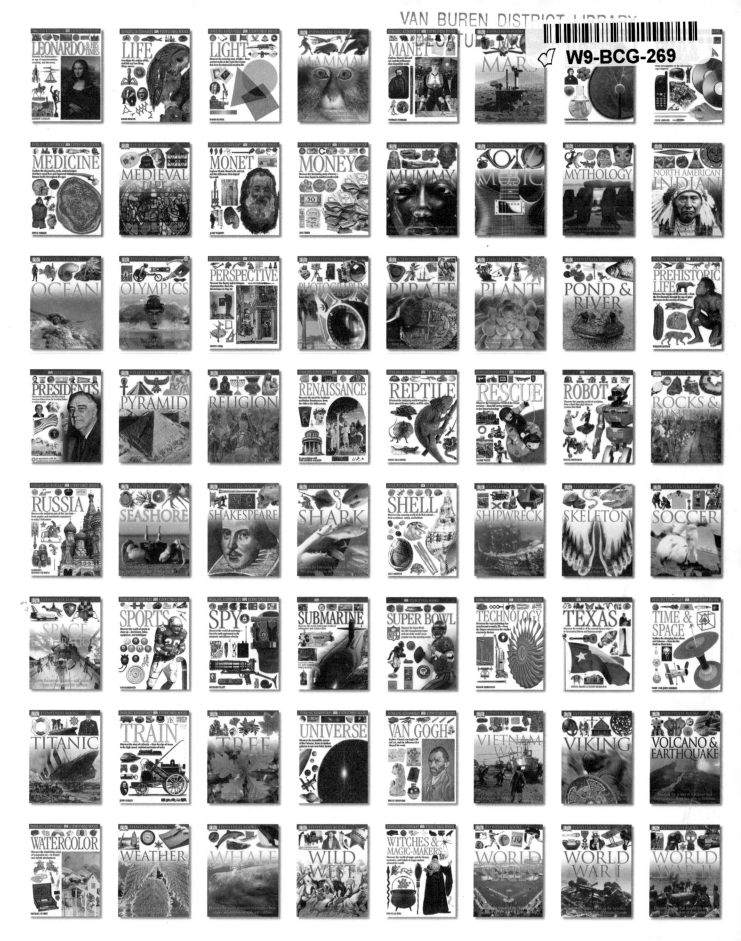

Eyewitness
FISH

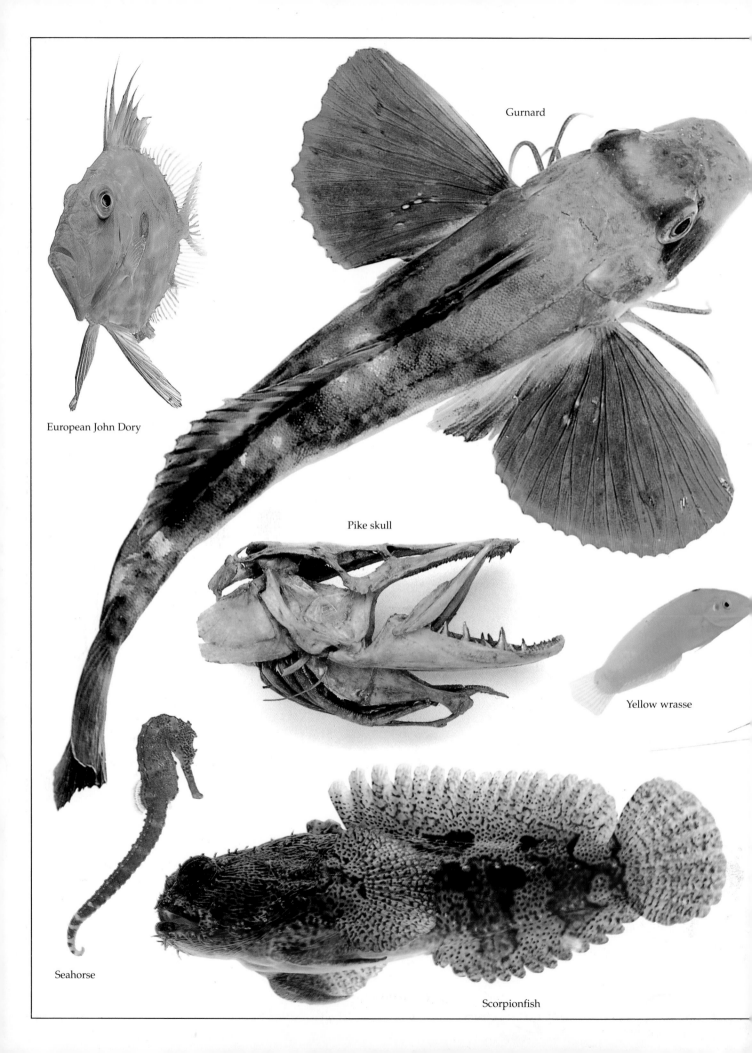

Gurnard

European John Dory

Pike skull

Yellow wrasse

Seahorse

Scorpionfish

Cuban hock

Royal gramma

Eyewitness
FISH

Written by
STEVE PARKER

Triggerfish

Catfish

Spiny boxfish

Thornback ray

Atlantic
blue tang

Yellow cichlid

DK

DK Publishing, Inc.

Twinspot wrasse

Birdnosed wrasse

DK

LONDON, NEW YORK, MUNICH,
MELBOURNE, and DELHI

Project editor Susan McKeever
Art editor Neville Graham
Senior editor Sophie Mitchell
Senior art editor Julia Harris
Editorial director Sue Unstead
Art director Anne-Marie Bulat
Special photography Dave King, Kim Taylor,
Jane Burton, and Colin Keates
Editorial consultant Gordon Howes,
the Natural History Museum, London

REVISED EDITION
Editors Elizabeth Hester, Laura Buller
Publishing director Beth Sutinis
Art director Dirk Kaufman
DTP designer Milos Orlovic
Production Chris Avgherinos, Ivor Parker

This Eyewitness ® Guide has been conceived by
Dorling Kindersley Limited and Editions Gallimard

This edition published in the United States in 2005
by DK Publishing, Inc.
375 Hudson Street, New York, NY 10014

05 06 07 08 09 10 9 8 7 6 5 4 3 2 1

A catalog record for this
book is available from
the Library of Congress.

ISBN 0-7566-1073-7 (HC)
0-7566-1074-5 (Library Binding)

Color reproduction by
Colourscan, Singapore
Printed in China by Toppan Printing Co.,
(Shenzhen) Ltd.

Discover more at
www.dk.com

Underside of gurnard

Banded pipefish

Ribbon eel

Contents

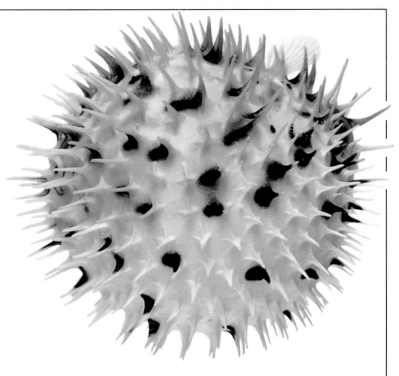

Fully inflated porcupine fish

6
What is a fish?
8
Inside a fish
10
The bones of a fish
12
Early fishes
14
Scale story
16
A riot of color
20
Amazing shapes
22
Pipes and horses
24
Changing faces
28
The art of swimming
30
Tails and fins
32
Fishes with legs
34
Fishes feeding
36
Food out of water
38
Scaring the enemy
40
Setting up house
42
Fish eggs
44
Attentive parents
46
Living in harmony

48
Snakes of the sea
50
Hiding places
52
Life on the move
54
Poisonous fishes
56
All about rays
58
The great warriors of the sea
62
Studying fishes
64
Did you know?
66
Fish tales
68
Find out more
70
Glossary
72
Index

What is a fish?

THE WORD "FISH" CONJURES UP different images for different people. Some people visualize a streamlined shark; others, a group of brightly colored tropical fishes darting through a coral reef. Yet others will (mistakenly) think of water-dwelling mammals, such as whales and dolphins. Fishes are in fact a vast and varied group of fascinating aquatic creatures, superbly designed for underwater life. There are three main fish groups (p. 9). Each group developed along different evolutionary pathways, as shown by their body form and internal structure. They are vastly different, but we can make a few generalizations. Most fishes live in water, breathe with their gills, have scales, and swim using their fins. All fishes are vertebrates, which means that they have a backbone, and an internal skeleton rather than an outside "shell," or exoskeleton. There are five main groups of vertebrates: fishes, amphibians, reptiles, birds, and mammals. Most people are aware of the variety within the last four groups. Yet there are about as many kinds, or species, of fishes (some 20,000) as there are in the other four groups put together!

The mythical mermaid, with a woman's body and a fish's tail, may have been the result of wishful thinking by sailors on long voyages

Fin rays support fin web

Lateral line

Two-lobed caudal fin ("tail," p. 30)

FISHY FEATURES
The basic fish shape is very streamlined for slipping smoothly through the water – tubelike, with a front end that tapers to a point. The common European carp has most of the typical "fishy features," although it is on the large side and can be up to 3 ft (1 m) long. The carp is "deeper" from back to belly than many species, which means that it is not a fast swimmer. There are two main types of fins: paired, (one on each side of the body) and median, or unpaired. The paired fins are the pectorals and pelvics, and they help with steering and maneuvering. The median fins are the dorsals (some species have up to three), the anal (or ventral), and the caudal fin – usually called the tail. The dorsal and anal fins give the fish stability, like the keel of a sailboat, while in most species the tail provides the power for moving forward.

Anal fin

Covering of slimy mucus over body helps fish to slip through water and protects against parasites

Right pelvic fin

Whale shark

Dwarf pygmy goby

BIG FISH, LITTLE FISH
Fishes vary in size more than any other group of vertebrates. The world's biggest fish is the whale shark, a harmless oceanic filter feeder which grows to 49 ft (15 m) long and weighs over 20 tons; the smallest is the Filipino dwarf pygmy goby, at only .3 in (8 mm) long.

Dwarf pygmy goby (actual size)

What is not a fish?

Some animals are thought of as "fishes" simply because they live in water, but they are not true fishes. Fish-shaped dolphins and seals are mammals and must come to the surface to breathe. Shellfish, like mussels and cuttlefish are in fact mollusks. "Nonfish" animals with fishy names include the crayfish and the spiny-skinned starfish, neither of which are fishes.

Bottle-nosed dolphin

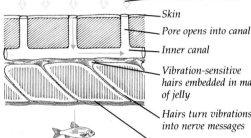
Atlantic cuttlefish

Dorsal fin (on the carp this is very long and has about 20 fin rays supporting it)

FEELING IN WATER
Water is an excellent carrier of sound vibrations. Fishes sense these mainly with their lateral line, a fluid-filled tube or canal that runs along each side of the body, under the skin. Vibrations pass into the canal via tiny pores in the skin and shake tiny lumps of jelly there, which stimulate nerve endings. The fish can "feel" water movements created by currents and other creatures.

Vibrations in water
Skin
Pore opens into canal
Inner canal
Vibration-sensitive hairs embedded in mass of jelly
Hairs turn vibrations into nerve messages
Sensory nerves to brain

Overlapping scales on body (p. 14)

Eye (many fishes have excellent eyesight)

Nostril

Horny lips

Mouth (for feeding and taking in water to "breathe")

Barbel (fleshy, touch-sensitive whisker)

Operculum (bony covering for gills)

Belly

Scales are almost transparent, letting deep silvery layers of skin show through and aiding camouflage

Right pectoral fin

FRESH OR SALT?
All water is not the same. Its saltiness has a great effect on a fish's internal chemistry. In rivers and lakes, fresh water is absorbed by a fish's body, so the fish must make large quantities of dilute urine to get rid of it. In the saltwater of the sea, the fish's body tends to lose water, so a marine fish drinks a lot and produces only a little, very concentrated urine. As a result, the vast majority of fishes can only live in either fresh water or saltwater. However, a few, like the salmon, leave the sea to swim up rivers and breed in fresh water. They are known as anadromous species. Eels do the opposite (p. 49) and are called catadromous.

Leaping salmon: making the perilous journey from sea to river

Pisces the fish is a sign of the Zodiac

Inside a fish

THE TYPICAL FISH has many of the body organs found in reptiles, birds, and even mammals like ourselves. A skeleton provides the internal framework (p. 10). The brain receives information about the outside world via sense organs such as the eyes and the lateral line (p. 7) and coordinates the complex movements of swimming, which are carried out by teams of muscles. Instead of the lungs of air-breathing animals, fishes have gills which do the same job – absorbing oxygen. The fish's heart pumps blood through a network of vessels, and its digestive system processes food into nutrients for growth and repair. Various glands make digestive juices and other body chemicals (hormones) that control development. There are also sexual organs for breeding (p. 40). The scientific study of fish is called ichthyology.

How fishes breathe

All animals, from eagles to fishes, need oxygen in order to survive. On land, of course, oxygen is in the air. Water contains oxygen, too, in a dissolved form. Fishes "breathe" in water using their gills. Water flows past the rich blood supply in the gills. Oxygen passes from the water through the thin gill membranes into the fish's blood, which then distributes it throughout the body.

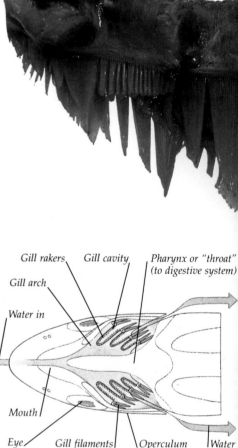

THE ADAPTABLE SWIM BLADDER
This develops as an outgrowth of the gut (intestine). In many bony fishes it controls buoyancy (top). In some tropical freshwater fishes the swim bladder is attached to the hearing organs and amplifies sounds (middle). Lungfishes have two swim bladders lined with blood vessels which absorb oxygen from swallowed air (bottom).

Swim bladders – front view (left), side view (right)

BONY FISH
Most of the internal organs of a typical bony fish like the perch are packed into the lower front half of the body. The rest of its insides consist of blocks of muscle that produce swimming movements. Some fishes, like carps, have a tightly coiled intestine in place of a stomach.

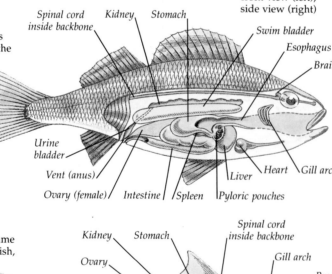

Spinal cord inside backbone · Kidney · Stomach · Swim bladder · Esophagus · Brain · Urine bladder · Vent (anus) · Ovary (female) · Intestine · Spleen · Pyloric pouches · Liver · Heart · Gill arch

Gill rakers · Gill cavity · Pharynx or "throat" (to digestive system) · Gill arch · Water in · Mouth · Eye · Gill filaments · Operculum (Gill cover) · Water out

WATER FLOW PAST THE GILLS *above*
Although most fishes take intermittent gulps of water, inside the gill chambers there is a fairly constant flow. A mouthful of water is taken in while the operculum (gill cover) shuts to keep water from escaping past it. The fish then closes its mouth and pressurizes the water within. This flows past the gills and pushes open the flaplike operculum on its way out. (In sharks, each gill arch has its own slitlike opening on the outside.) In fast swimmers such as tunas and mackerels, the pressure of water due to the fish's forward movement is enough to keep a current of water flowing past the gills.

CARTILAGINOUS FISH
A shark has roughly the same internal organs as a bony fish, except that it lacks a swim bladder. Also, near the end of its intestine is a corkscrew-shaped structure known as a spiral valve, which probably increases the surface area for absorbing nutrients.

Kidney · Stomach · Spinal cord inside backbone · Ovary · Gill arch · Brain · Cloaca (outlet for feces, urine, and eggs or sperm) · Intestine · Spleen · Liver · Esophagus · Heart · Pharynx

JAWLESS FISH
The hagfish's digestive tract is little more than a straight tube, from mouth to anus. Also, it breathes through gill pouches, which are internal pockets linked to the pharynx and lined with fine blood vessels, instead of through fish gills.

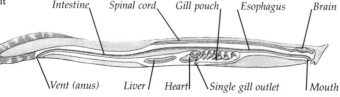

Intestine · Spinal cord · Gill pouch · Esophagus · Brain · Vent (anus) · Liver · Heart · Single gill outlet · Mouth

THE GILL ARCHES

The gills of a big, active fish such as a tuna must take a lot of oxygen from the water to power the fish's muscular activity. Under each gill cover are four gills; each gill is supported by a curved or V-shaped bony arch. On each arch is a double row of gill filaments, and each filament is made of many leaflike folds called lamellae. This gives a large surface area for absorbing oxygen – up to 10 times the area of the fish's body.

Gill filaments (toward rear), made of leaflike folds called lamellae

Stiff gill rakers (face forward) filter in clean water passing over gills

Bony support of gill arch

Tuna fish gill shown at slightly bigger than life size

BREATHING OUT OF WATER

Some fishes can survive in warm, still, oxygen-poor waters by gulping air and absorbing its oxygen in various ways. The 13 ft (4 m) pirarucu (arapaima), a giant fish of the Amazon region, gulps air into its swim bladder which is linked to the pharynx (throat) where it absorbs oxygen. The Indian snakehead takes air into the folded, blood-vessel-lined pouches of its pharynx.

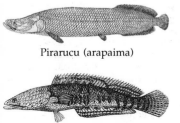

Pirarucu (arapaima)

Indian snakehead

THE MAIN GROUPS OF LIVING FISHES

Jawless fishes (agnathans)		lamprey, hagfish	About 45 species
Cartilaginous fishes (chondrichthians)		shark, ray, skate	About 600 species
	Sharks and rays (elasmobranchs)		
	Chimaeras (holocephalans)	rabbitfish, ratfish	20 species
Bony fishes (osteichthians)		coelacanth	1 species
Lobe-finned fishes (sarcopterygians)	Tassel-finned fishes (crossopterygians)	African lungfish Australian lungfish	7 species
	Lungfishes (dipnoi)		
Ray-finned fishes (actinopterygians)	Chondrosteans	sturgeon, paddlefish, bichir	36 species
	Holosteans	gar, bowfin	8 species
	Teleosts	perch, carp, and thousands of other "modern" bony fishes	Over 25,000 species altogether

MAIN GROUPS OF FISHES

During the evolution of fishes, thousands of species have become extinct, some leaving fossils which give clues as to how present-day groups are related (p. 12). Some rare and obscure species are placed in groups all on their own since they are the only living relatives of fishes now extinct. Some, like the lungfish, may be the ancestors of the first land vertebrates.

The bones of a fish

ALL FISHES HAVE INTERNAL SKELETONS, like us. Most fish skeletons are made of bone (bony fish, or teleosts) and have three main regions: the skull – made up of a series of plate-shaped bones with supports – which houses the brain, and from which the jaws and gill arches hang; the vertebral column, or backbone, which bears the spine and ribs; and the "fin skeleton" – the bones and rods which anchor and support the various fins and tail. Some fishes, such as sturgeon, have skeletons of both cartilage and bone. They are called primitive bony fishes. Sharks and rays have skeletons made up of cartilage instead of bone and are called cartilaginous fishes.

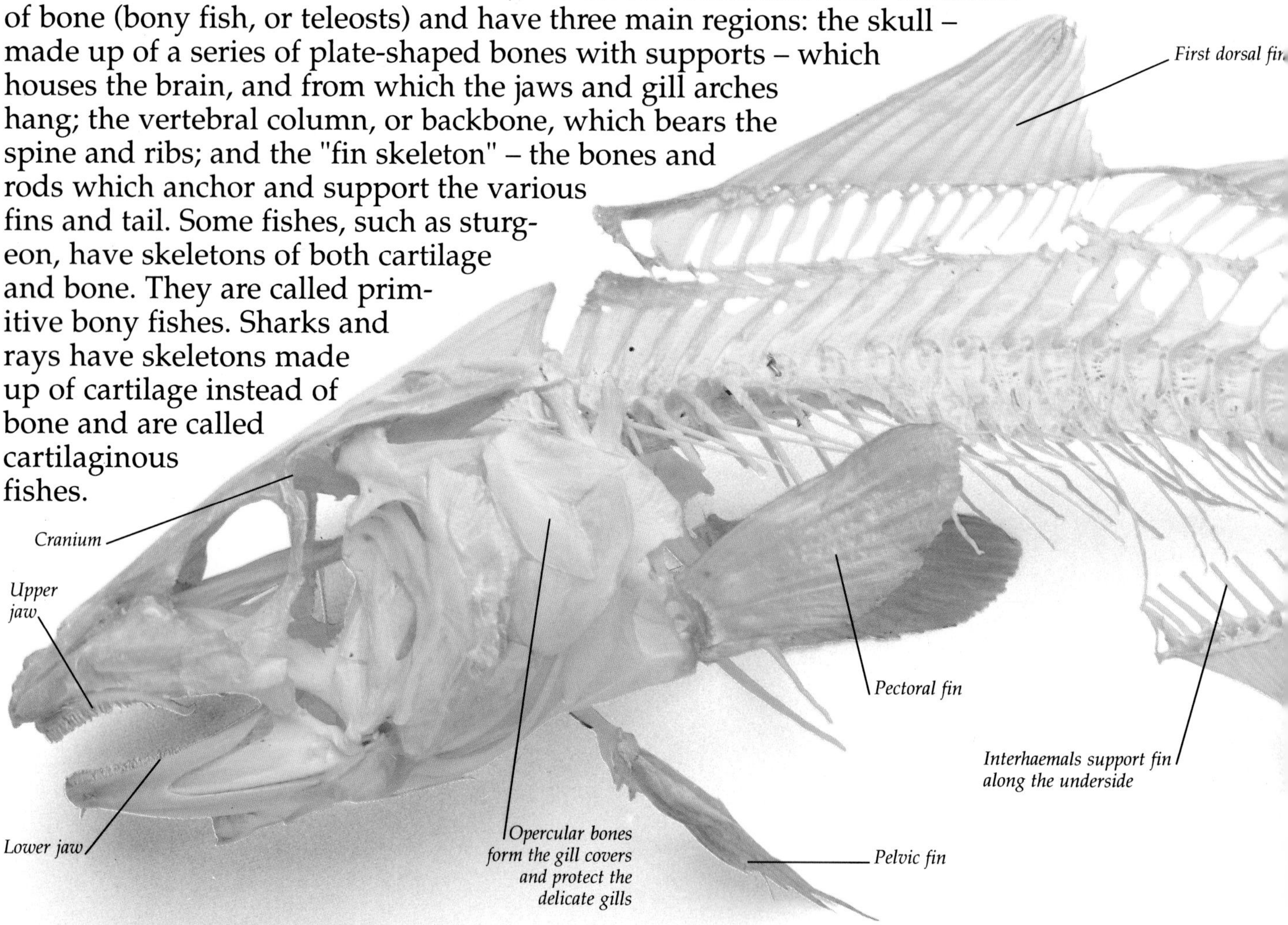

First dorsal fin

Cranium

Upper jaw

Lower jaw

Opercular bones form the gill covers and protect the delicate gills

Pectoral fin

Interhaemals support fin along the underside

Pelvic fin

A load of old bones

Like most successful groups of animals, fishes have evolved into various shapes and sizes from coping with different lifestyles. The shape of the internal skeleton evolves accordingly. Regions of the skeleton may gradually get bigger to support and enlarge part of the body, or shrink away to almost nothing when their framework and rigidity are no longer useful. Some unusual parts of skeletons are shown to the right.

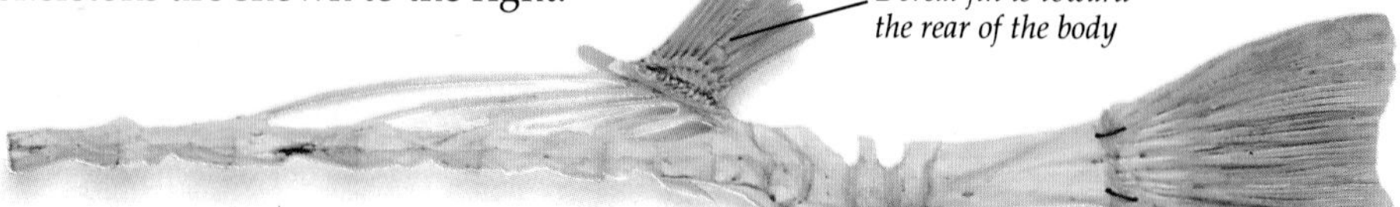

BASKER'S BACKBONE
The basking shark is the world's second-largest fish, next to the whale shark. Since it is a shark, its skeleton is made mainly of cartilage. This is the central portion, or centrum, of a vertebra; it is strengthened by a network of mineral-laced fibers.

Centrum is strengthened by a network of fibers

Dorsal fin is toward the rear of the body

TRUNKFISH TRUNK
The backbone of the trunkfish has long rods supporting its dorsal fin, which is toward the rear of the body, near the tail. This fish's body is covered in a protective armor of "chain mail," formed from bony six-sided scales. It swims slowly, using only its fins and tail, because its body is too stiff to flex.

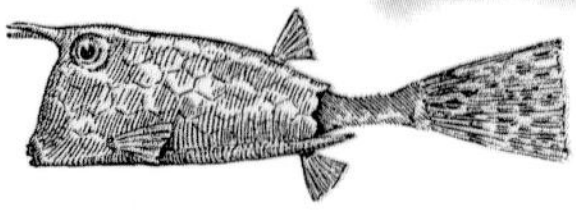

Trunkfish

STOUT, NOT SPEEDY
The backbone of the cascadura, a South American armored catfish, is stout and inflexible. This fish has rows of overlapping bony plates along its body, which slows it down but gives it protection.

THE FISH'S FRAMEWORK

This well-preserved skeleton of an Atlantic cod is typical of the great majority of teleosts, or "true" bony fishes (p. 10). There are two main types of fish bones. Cartilage bones form their shapes first in cartilage, then change into bone as the fish develops. Dermal bones develop from layers in the skin (*derma* means "skin"). The cod is a valuable food fish, and its rows of sharp teeth identify it as a predator. It primarily eats other fishes such as mackerel and herring, but it will snap at almost anything. People who fish for cod have found strange things in cod stomachs, including a partridge, turnips, and even a leather-bound book!

Atlantic cod

Interneurals support the fins along the back

Second dorsal fin – unlike many fishes, the cod has three dorsal fins

EVER-GREEN BONES
Marine garfishes are often caught by people who fish. But people are discouraged from eating them by the strange bright green color of the skeleton. No one knows why garfishes have green bones – the color lasts even after boiling.

Spine

Lepidotrichs, or fin rays, support all dorsal and anal fins

Caudal fin (tail)

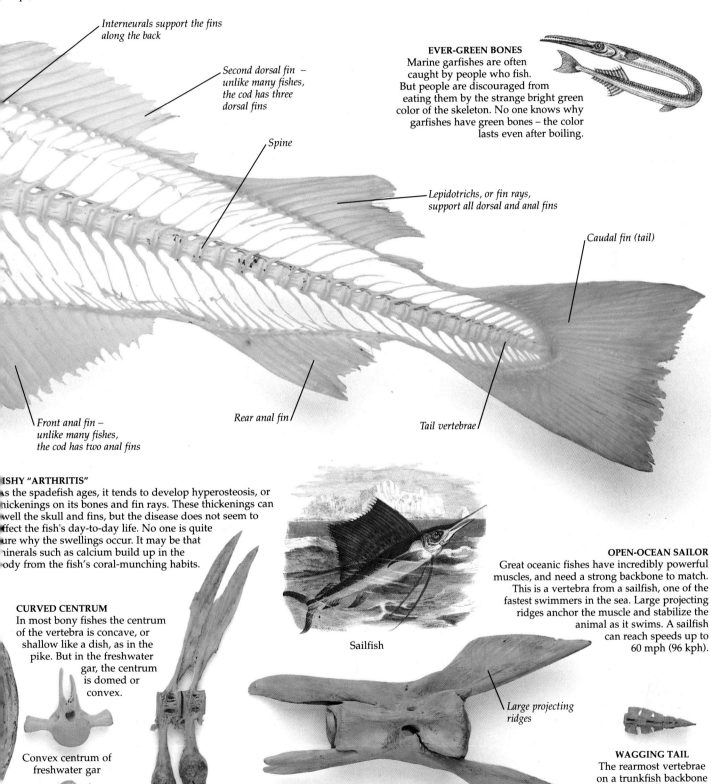

Rear anal fin

Tail vertebrae

Front anal fin – unlike many fishes, the cod has two anal fins

FISHY "ARTHRITIS"
As the spadefish ages, it tends to develop hyperosteosis, or thickenings on its bones and fin rays. These thickenings can swell the skull and fins, but the disease does not seem to affect the fish's day-to-day life. No one is quite sure why the swellings occur. It may be that minerals such as calcium build up in the body from the fish's coral-munching habits.

CURVED CENTRUM
In most bony fishes the centrum of the vertebra is concave, or shallow like a dish, as in the pike. But in the freshwater gar, the centrum is domed or convex.

Convex centrum of freshwater gar

Concave centrum of pike

Sailfish

OPEN-OCEAN SAILOR
Great oceanic fishes have incredibly powerful muscles, and need a strong backbone to match. This is a vertebra from a sailfish, one of the fastest swimmers in the sea. Large projecting ridges anchor the muscle and stabilize the animal as it swims. A sailfish can reach speeds up to 60 mph (96 kph).

Large projecting ridges

Vertebrae showing characteristic swelling from bone disease

WAGGING TAIL
The rearmost vertebrae on a trunkfish backbone (see far left) have keels for muscle attachment. The tail is flexed from side to side at its base.

Early fishes

NEARLY 500 MILLION YEARS AGO, the first fishes swam in the earth's waters. They had no jaws, fins, or scales like the fishes of today. But early fishes did have a kind of backbone. The backbone sets apart vertebrates (animals with backbones) such as birds, mammals, reptiles, amphibians, and the fishes themselves, from the invertebrates (animals without backbones) such as insects, spiders, and worms. The backbone formed a firm yet flexible central brace against which powerful muscles could pull, to propel the creature along. Fish skeletons fossilized very well, partly because they were made of hard bone. As the primitive fishes developed further, another new trait evolved – jaws. This was a major advance, since jawless creatures are mostly restricted to sucking or scraping at food. Jaws enabled fishes to bite and chew and were an enormous success. Today, all fishes except the lampreys and hagfishes have jaws of some kind.

FISHY LANDSCAPE
The first fishes with jaws appeared 435 million year ago, during the Silurian Period. This strange scene shows where they might have swum.

Sharklike fin

TIME CHART SHOWING EVOLUTION OF THE FISHES

Millions of years ago
500   400   300 Present day

Jawless fishes

Sharks and rays

Fossil bony fishes

Modern bony fishes

Coelacanths

Bony shield protected fish

TINY SPINY
Ischnacanthus was an acanthodian, or "spiny shark." These ancient fish were somewhat sharklike in shape, and each fin had a strong spine along its front edge. They flourished about 400-350 million years ago and then gradually died out.

JAWLESS WONDER
Cephalaspis belonged to a group of extinct fishes called the osteostracans, which were among the first fishes to appear on Earth. This fossil is nearly 400 million years old. Most early fishes like these did not possess jaws. They had round, fleshy mouths for sucking. The large, bony shield protected the fish's head and gills. These types of fishes were only about 4 in (10 cm) long.

Restoration of Cephalaspis

FIRST OF THE RAY-FINS
The palaeonisciforms were the first of the bony, "ray-finned" fishes (p. 9) which now make up the vast majority of fish species. At first the rodlike fin rays (lepidotrichs) were parallel to the fish's body, but gradually they splayed out to make a fan shape as in the fins of most modern fishes. In this fine fossil of *Palaeoniscus*, from 250 million years ago, the sculpted individual body scales are clearly visible.

Restoration of Palaeoniscus

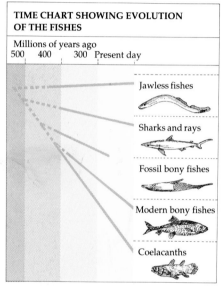

Sculpted individual body scales

Cartilage struts

Scales

ROUNDED HOLOSTEAN
Dapedium dates from the Lower Jurassic period, some 190 million years ago. It was a member of the holostean group, common at the time (p. 9). Holosteans had a fully developed backbone, but the rest of the bony skeleton was poorly developed. Today there are still some living species of holostean, including the gars of North and Central America. The giant gar grows to more than 10 ft (3 m) in length and hunts smaller fishes for food.

Large predatory mouth

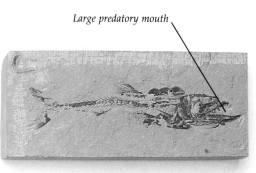

THE RISE OF THE TELEOSTS
Eurypholis has the streamlined shape, large mouth, and sharp teeth of a hunter. It is a teleost, or "true" bony fish (p. 9). Teleosts make up the great majority of fish species alive today. These agile and adaptable creatures rose to success some 200-100 million years ago.

This restoration of *Eusthenopteron* shows the bones of the head and internal skeleton

FINS TO LEGS
The slim, predatory *Eusthenopteron* was a primitive lobe-finned fish. Some lobe fins are thought to be related to coelacanths and lungfishes and so are on the ancestral line that gave rise to land-living vertebrates (tetrapods). However, *Eusthenopteron* itself was not a tetrapod ancestor, but merely a fish adapted to the conditions of its time.

ALMOST THERE
Teleost fishes such as the small *Stichocentrus* gradually took over the waters from the many fish groups that had lived before (p. 9). With their bony inner skeletons, flexible fins, efficient jaws, and lightweight scales, they had come a long way from the jawless, heavily armored, tanklike versions such as *Cephalaspis*.

TRUT-FILLED 'INGS
ays have skeletons ade of cartilage (p. 9), hich is softer and decays ore quickly than bone so is fossilized less often. herefore we know less bout the evolution of ys and sharks than we about bony fishes. his specimen is a *eliobatis*, a kind of ingray. It displays the dozens of cartilage struts (supports) in its "wings" (pectoral fins). Rays today are much like those that lived millions of years ago.

Flipper-like fins

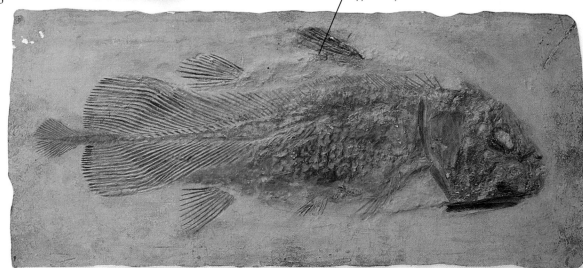

Famous fish

In 1938 scientists were startled by the discovery in South Africa of a coelacanth. Many fossil coelacanths were known, dating back to nearly 400 million years ago. However, experts had thought they had died out 80 million years ago. But it seemed local people had been catching them for years. They had even been using their scales to roughen punctured bicycle-tire inner tubes before sticking on a patch. More than 100 coelacanths have since been caught, and they have also been filmed swimming near the Comoro Islands, off southeast Africa.

The coelacanth today – still alive and swimming

Scale story

Most fishes are covered with a layer of thin, transparent plates called scales, which overlap like shingles on a roof. There are four main types of scale: cycloid and ctenoid, which are found on true bony fish; ganoid, found on primitive bony fish; and placoid, found on some cartilaginous fish. Ctenoid scales have tiny teeth along the edge; fishes with these scales, such as bass and perch, feel rough to the touch. Cycloid scales have a smooth surface and are found on carp and salmon. Gar have ganoid scales, which are shiny, hard, and diamond shaped. Sharks and most rays have placoid scales, which look like tiny teeth or thorns.

Large reflective scales along lateral line

Ventral fin

Pelvic fin

STURGEON'S SCUTES
As they evolved, over the past 135 million years, sturgeons gradually lost most of their scales. All that remain are five rows of large flat scutes (bony plates) along the length of the body. A scute from a big sturgeon can be as big as 4 in (10 cm) across.

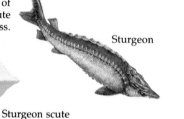

Sturgeon

Sturgeon scute

NONSLIP GRIP
For centuries people have appreciated the rough texture of shark skin, using it as a natural sand-paper or nonslip sword grip. Shark and ray scales, called denticles or placoid scales, are different from bony fish scales. They are generally tooth-shaped and each one has a bony core fixed in the tough skin and a backward-sloping spine. Stroke a shark the wrong way, and you could severely scrape your own skin.

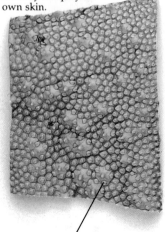

Diamond-shaped interlocking scales

Side view of gar scales showing slight overlap

CHAIN-MAIL SCALES
The North American gar has the closely fitting, diamond-shaped scales that its many extinct relatives had. These ganoid scales are linked by fibers to form a strong and inflexible suit of chain-mail armor. Early European settlers in North America used tough gar skin to cover their ploughs.

Garfis

COELACANTH SUIT
The coelacanth (p. 13) has a different kind of scale from most other fishes. Each scale is a bony plate with small toothlike spines, somewhat like shark denticles, and overlaps the scale next to it.

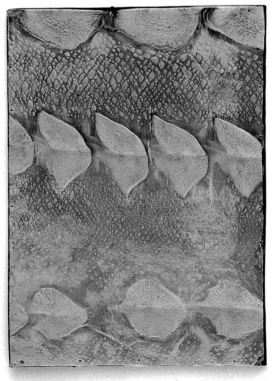

Shark denticle

Sturgeon skin showing three rows of scutes

Mirror carp

SHINING SCALES
With its large reflective scales, the mirror carp, a type of common carp, is an unusual sight. Its scales appear mainly along its lateral line – leaving the rest of the body "naked." Silvery reflective skin grains show clearly underneath its cycloid scales. The leather carp, another type of common carp, has no scales at all.

COUNTING SCALES
In most fishes, scales run downward and toward the rear of the body in diagonally sloping rows. Counting the exact numbers of rows helps to identify a fish accurately. The number of scales along the length of the body (lateral line) gives the number of diagonal rows. The number of scales from back to belly (along the transverse line) gives the number of horizontal rows.

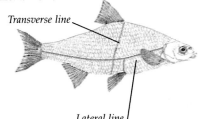

Transverse line

Lateral line

Parts of body without scales

ON A LARGE SCALE
Tarpon scales are among the largest of the cycloid bony fish scales, each being more than 2 in (5 cm) across. They are smooth and are often used to make decorative jewelry. The tarpon, a powerful predator, is similar to the earliest true bony fishes.

Tarpon scale

Tarpon

THE RIGHT SCALE
The carp scale is a good example of the leptoid scale found on most bony fishes. Each scale has two platelike layers – a bony one and a thin fibrous one. Its root, or front end, is embedded in a pocket in the lower layer of dermis (skin), and the other end is free.

HOW OLD?
Under the microscope, a carp scale shows growth rings, like a tree trunk. Bony fishes have roughly the same number of scales throughout their life. Several widely spaced rings on the scales indicate a season of rapid growth for the fish.

COMBED SCALE
Angelfish scales have tiny teeth, like a miniature comb, along the exposed edge. They are called ctenoid or "comblike" scales.

Growth rings on magnified carp scale

Spines in skin become erect when porcupine fish is annoyed or scared

THORNY CAT
The thorny catfish has a single row of large pointed scutes, like rose thorns, along each side of the body. It also has a strong skull that extends into a bony plate that protects the neck region. Its large fins are edged with toothed spines. Not surprisingly, these South American river-dwellers have earned the nickname of "touch-me-not-fish."

Thorny catfish (a type of armored catfish)

Row of scutes with sharp thorns

SPINY SCALES
This close-up shows the prickly spines of the porcupine fish. Even laid flat, the kite-shaped bases of the spines fit tightly to give good protection. When the fish is scared, it puffs itself up to erect the spines (p. 38).

A riot of color

FISHES HAVE EVOLVED almost every imaginable color and pattern. This is very useful for the fish in a variety of ways. Color can camouflage a fish from both predator and prey: smooth silvery greens, blues, and browns camouflage some species in open water; a riot of brilliant reds, yellows, and blues conceals others among the equally splendid colors of a coral reef. Spots, stripes, and patches "disrupt" or break up a fish's outline, confusing predators. Color and pattern also help a fish chase away intruders from its territory. When breeding, some fishes' colors become brighter, which attracts potential mates.

Lateral line

Large "pearl" scales

Eye stripe

Disruptive vertical stripe on tail

PEARLY SCALES
In the pearl-scaled butterflyfish, the yellow and orange colors typical of butterflyfishes are confined to its tail end. The large pearly scales create a rainbow effect of color, and the fish's eye is camouflaged by a black stripe.

Barbels for finding way and food in muddy water

Clown loach

HIDING IN THE SHADOWS
Loaches swim mostly near the bottom. The clown loach likes to hide among lake-bottom plants, where its broad dark stripes resemble fallen branches and the shadows of plant stems.

Forceps fish

Long, thin forceps-like mouth for nibbling in crevices

False eyespot on dorsal fin may distract predators

False eyespot

TAILS YOU LOSE
The forceps fish has a false eyespot near its tail base. As a predator approaches from behind, intending to attack the "head," the forceps fish swishes its fins and darts off the other way.

Royal gramma

Eye hidden by stripe

REGAL PURPLE
The royal gramma gets its name from its startlingly bright "royal purple" front end. This species is a cave dweller, so its coloration probably does not act as camouflage. But it is very territorial, and the bright hues probably make it very visible as it chases away competitors.

ZEBRA IN THE GRASS
Instead of hiding upright as one long, thin stem of waterweed, like the snake pipefish (p. 23), this banded pipefish hides horizontally – looking like 28 stems!

Dark spot on dorsal fin

Transparent tail makes fish look two-ended

GROWING COLORS
As this young French angelfish grows, the four vertical off-white bars will deepen to vivid yellow and the rest of the body will darken.

French angelfish

Pale flecks on body will darken to solid olive green

EYE SURPRISE
Flicking up its dorsal fin, the one-spot yellow wrasse reveals an eyelike dark spot against the brilliant yellow background – a surprise for any predator.

DESIGNER'S NIGHTMARE
A white mustard-lined forehead, zebra colored zigzags fading into a bright yellow tail, and a false eyespot on the rear of the dorsal fin – it is difficult to imagine a more varied patterning than on this golden butterflyfish, which lives in warm Australian seas.

...ye hidden by ...ead stripe

Golden butterflyfish

Gap below eyespot, between rear of dorsal fin and tail fin, resembles a "mouth"

SPOT THE WRASSE
Ocean wrasses are one of the most colorful of fish groups. This red, white, and green wrasse cruises through seaweed fronds; its spots and splotches draw attention away from the overall fishy outline.

First spine in dorsal fin can be locked erect by second "trigger" spine

Eye is tinted red

Eye concealed by dark facial stripe

Spotted triggerfish

DIRTY RED
Scattered dark scales on the Cuban hock's body and on the tips of its dorsal and pectoral fins help to give the fish a slightly "dirty" appearance, perhaps aiding camouflage. The eye is tinted red and matches the fish's upper body. This species also has fine decorative fin rays.

Cuban hock

ALL DRESSED UP
Be a predator. Close your eyes. Now open them to look at the spotted triggerfish for a second, then close them again. With such a dramatic set of contrasting and broken patterns, it is difficult to prepare yourself for an attack on this species.

Tail remains yellow as in young fish

Atlantic blue tang

GETTING THE BLUES
The Atlantic blue tang, a member of the surgeonfish group from warm Atlantic coral reefs, is mostly yellow-colored as a young fish. As the fish matures, the deep, rich blue gradually spreads from the front of the body to the rear.

Red flaglike tail may be used to startle predators

...ebra pipefish

Mandarin fish

SEA BED DOODLE
"Scribblefish" is a nickname for the mandarin fish, which frequents coral reefs and rocks across the eastern Indian and western Pacific oceans. Like its relative the dragonet, the male mandarin fish has long spines on the first dorsal fin.

Blue-ringed "eyespot"

...ague dark bands ...un along back

Spine on gill cover is typical of the angelfish group

...OT SO YELLOW
...n close examination, the ...ins and scales of the yellow ...ichlid show subtle shades of ...ream, gray, orange, and brown.

Yellow cichlid

BLUE BANDED
The striking electric blue bands of the blue-ringed angelfish are a strong visual signal to nearby members of the same species. However, the almost invisible tail disrupts the general fish shape.

17

Continued on next page

Cutting down on color

Fishes from the world's cooler waters, and those living in the open ocean, have more muted colors and patterns compared to the species of tropical lakes and coral reefs. Many that swim near the surface have "countershading": a darker back and paler belly. Light from above brightens the fish's back and shadows its undersurface – and so the fish "disappears" into the surrounding water.

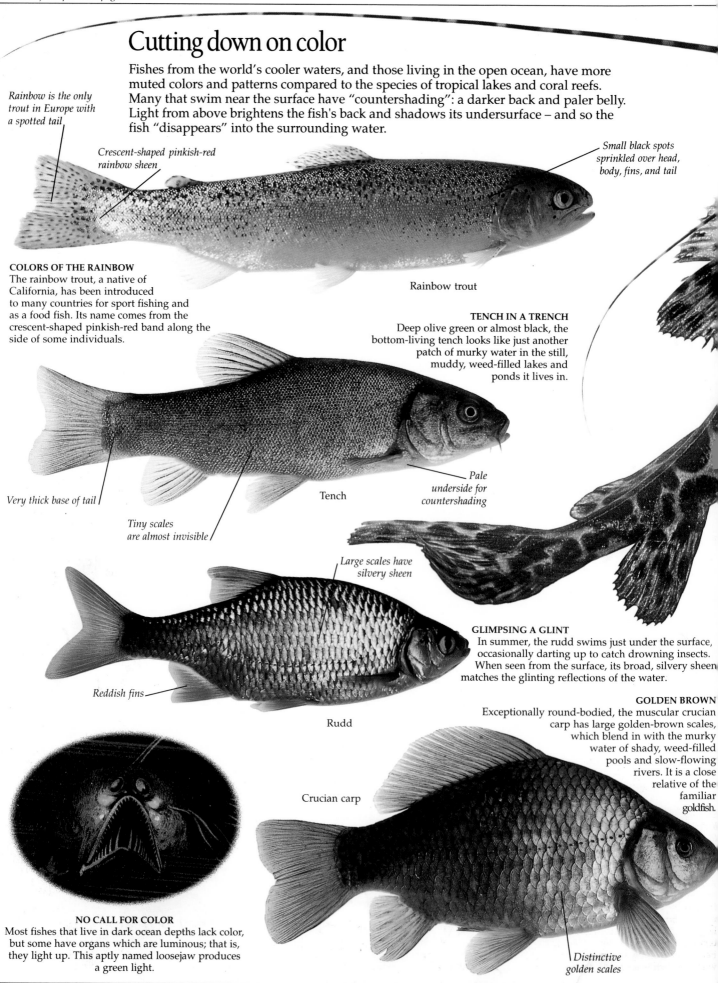

Rainbow is the only trout in Europe with a spotted tail

Crescent-shaped pinkish-red rainbow sheen

Small black spots sprinkled over head, body, fins, and tail

COLORS OF THE RAINBOW
The rainbow trout, a native of California, has been introduced to many countries for sport fishing and as a food fish. Its name comes from the crescent-shaped pinkish-red band along the side of some individuals.

Rainbow trout

TENCH IN A TRENCH
Deep olive green or almost black, the bottom-living tench looks like just another patch of murky water in the still, muddy, weed-filled lakes and ponds it lives in.

Very thick base of tail

Pale underside for countershading

Tench

Tiny scales are almost invisible

Large scales have silvery sheen

GLIMPSING A GLINT
In summer, the rudd swims just under the surface, occasionally darting up to catch drowning insects. When seen from the surface, its broad, silvery sheen matches the glinting reflections of the water.

GOLDEN BROWN
Exceptionally round-bodied, the muscular crucian carp has large golden-brown scales, which blend in with the murky water of shady, weed-filled pools and slow-flowing rivers. It is a close relative of the familiar goldfish.

Reddish fins

Rudd

Crucian carp

NO CALL FOR COLOR
Most fishes that live in dark ocean depths lack color, but some have organs which are luminous; that is, they light up. This aptly named loosejaw produces a green light.

Distinctive golden scales

Long barbels for feeling the way along the dark bottom

Schooling mark helps young of a species identify each other

Freshwater catfish

Fish gets its name from dorsal fin, which stands up like a top hat

FLYING THE FLAG
The flag cichlid is one of the many varieties of festive cichlids (also called barred or festa cichlids). Some South American cichlids have been bred to get fish of all colors of the rainbow.

High-hat drumfish

BLACK CAT
Catfishes, so-called because of their whisker-like barbels, are usually darkly colored. This freshwater catfish from South America, like most of its relatives, lives mostly on or near the bottom. When it does swim to the surface, its splotched belly mimics the dappled effect of light on water.

Vivid stripes

SOUND, THEN SIGHT
Drumfishes or "croakers" are so-called because they make drumming and knocking sounds, especially to locate potential mates. These noises carry far underwater; as the fishes come closer to each other, eyesight takes over and they recognize one another by visual signals, like the vivid stripes on this high-hat drum.

TOP AND BOTTOM
The blue shark, which swims near the surface, is light on its underside and dark on top. The carpet shark lies on the bottom and blends in well with weeds and rocks.

Blue shark

Carpet shark (wobbegong)

Panther grouper

Large black spots on body

LURKING HUNTER
Named after the big cat, the panther, or spotted, grouper behaves similarly to the land predator around rocks and reefs. In its speckly natural habitat, the reef, the pattern of black spots on the whitish body becomes hard to see, but out of its natural habitat, it is highly visible.

Red eye

Sensory barbels to locate food in mud

Red mullet

RED WHEN DEAD
By day, the red mullet from European seas has a reddish-brown back and yellow lower body stripes. But at night it takes on a more marbled appearance. People who catch them marvel at the brilliant shining red that develops when the fish is stressed – that is, when it is caught and killed.

Yellow stripes along lower flank

GREEN SHEEN
The mackerel's countershading – a dark metallic green-blue back and a pale underside – makes the fish hard to see as it swims and feeds near the ocean's surface.

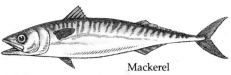

Mackerel

Amazing shapes

MOST FISHES ARE the usual "fish" shape, like the cod (p. 10). But there are endless variations on the theme. Long, slim, arrow-like fishes such as the gars are super-streamlined for quick dashes out of hiding. Other species are built more for surprise attack than for speed, like the squat, flat anglerfish which sits on the bottom and awaits its catch. Thin, deep-bodied fishes like the angelfishes are flexible and can slip between plant stems and coral formations. Shape, like color, helps to camouflage a fish. Waving fins may look like flowing plant leaves, and the entire body might resemble a plant, or even another animal.

DEEP-SEA ROCKET PLANE
Lurking in the depths of the North Atlantic is Harriott's longnose chimaera, a holocephalan (p. 8) that grows to 3 ft (1 m) long. With its long, thin snout and tail, and winglike pectoral fins, it looks a little like a space rocket.

THINLY DISGUISED
Head on, the European John Dory's extremely slim outline (left) is hard to spot as it moves slowly toward its prey. But from the side the John Dory looks disk-shaped. Disk-shaped fishes swim more slowly than streamlined models and tend to stalk their prey rather than chase it. The John Dory is well protected by the sets of stout spines in front of its dorsal and anal fins.

Rabbitfish

RABBIT'S TEETH, RAT'S TAIL
The rabbitfish's name was inspired by its rounded snout, which bears large cutting teeth, like the "buck" teeth of a rabbit. It is also called a chimaera, which was a grotesque monster of Greek mythology.

ELEPHANT'S SNOUT
Mormyrids, or elephant-trunk fishes, usually have a down curved mouth and nose for probing in the mud for food. (The head skeleton is shown on page 34). Peters' elephant-trunk fish has a relatively short "snout."

Dorsal fin set well back

Peduncle (narrow caudal region) – useful for getting in and out of tight places

Elephant-trunk fish

"Trunk" curves downward

John Dory – side view

Pelvic fins held edge on to minimize shape

Fins drawn out into fine filaments

Bars on body resemble reed stems

John Dory's minimal outline seen from front

Freshwater angelfish

Eye concealed by dark stripe

Dorsal fin set far back along body

Long jaws carry sharp teeth

Bars along side conceal fish among weeds and reeds

Longnose gar

STRAIGHT AS AN ARROW
Fully streamlined, the longnose gar from North American fresh waters can move very fast – but only in short bursts. It ambushes prey by dashing from its grassy hideout. (Its diamond-shaped scales are shown on page 14.)

AMAZING GRACE
The angelfish lives in slow-flowing South American rivers. Its crescent shape, body bars, and softly waving fins blend perfectly with the current-curved waterweeds. This species is a member of the cichlid group. The similar shaped saltwater French angelfish is on page 16.

Stout spines on back

FLYING HATCHET
The silver hatchetfish, with its extra-deep belly, can leap from the water while beating its large pectoral fins and "fly" short distances, skimming the surface. The fish got its name because of its resemblance to a hatchet (small hand ax). This is a freshwater fish from South America; a different type of hatchetfish lives in the deep sea.

Large pectoral fins flap as fish "flies"

Flat back – fish hangs just under surface waiting for flies

Freshwater hatchetfish

Deep body

Spines always held erect

Legend has it that dark spot on side is St. Pèter's thumbprint

LIVING IN A BOX
Like the porcupine fish (p. 38), the spiny boxfish has an angular body formed from flat, bony plates. Its spines, which are always erect, give added protection.

Fish can inflate its body with water

Flat body hugs rock

SEASHORE SUCKER
The clingfish's sucker-like pectoral fins and flat body allow it to stick to near-shore rocks.

HIDING IN SPINES
Shrimpfishes swim vertically among sea urchin spines. The narrow shape and black body stripe provide fine camouflage.

Clingfish

Humped silvery body looks like a knife

Clown knifefish

Spines in front of anal fin

GONE FISHIN'
The wide, flat, knobby body of the harlequin frogfish (a type of anglerfish) is suited to sitting on the sea bed, waiting for victims to approach the "rod and lure," which are a modified ray of the dorsal fin.

Sharp bony edge on underside

Shrimpfish

BLADE-SHAPED BODY
Knifefishes, such as this clown knifefish, have a long, slim, deep body shaped like a carving knife. The long anal fin joins with the caudal (tail) fin and provides propulsion.

Harlequin frogfish

Knifefish swims by moving long anal fin

Sharp spine under tail

Cowfish – front view, showing cowlike facial features

Protective spines look like horns of a cow

COW-HORNED AND COW-EYED
The cowfish is in the boxfish group (see above). Plates of bone under the skin form a rigid shell with only the mouth, eyes, gills, fins, and ventral opening on its outside.

Flat bony plates on underside

Cowfish – side view

Pipes and horses

THE HEAD OF A CHESS PIECE, the tail of a monkey, a ridged body that seems carved from wood, eyes like a chameleon, and a father who becomes pregnant. This describes the seahorse, which doesn't look like a fish at all. It swims upright, propelled by a waving dorsal fin. The small pectoral fins help to steer the animal as it glides along. There are no pelvic or tail fins at all. But there is a tail – tapering, muscular, and prehensile (grasping) – able to grip seaweed stems while the seahorse watches for food. In the same fish family, and almost as strange looking, is the pipefish. Pipefishes also swim mainly with their dorsal fins, and, like seahorses, are well protected by a casing of bony plates. Perhaps the strangest thing about these creatures is that the females lay their eggs "in" the males. Each male has a fold of skin or pocket-like pouch. Here the eggs develop into fully formed baby seahorses.

Orange sea whip coral

Dorsal fin

Platelike scales

Head set at right angles to body

Caribbean seahorse

Prehensile (grasping) tail

Tubelike sucking mouth

Jointed bony rings encircle tail

CORALLED HORSES
Three seahorses decorate a piece of gorgonia coral (orange sea whip). There are about 35 seahorse species around the world. The large one in the middle is from the Caribbean, and the two smaller yellow seahorses come from the Indian and Pacific oceans. However, color is no accurate guide, for most seahorses can change hues in minutes, from black or gray to bright yellow or orange. The seahorse hunts mainly by sight, sucking tiny water creatures such as baby fishes and shellfish into its tubular mouth. Its eyes can turn independently to view two scenes at once – one eye searching for food, perhaps, while the other watches out for predators. The seahorse can remain still for long periods, secured by its prehensile tail and well camouflaged among weeds or corals. Only its swiveling eyes may give it away.

22

PREGNANT FATHER

As the breeding season approaches, the male seahorse's pouch, in the front of his lower abdomen, becomes swollen and ready to receive eggs. The female lays up to 200 eggs in the pouch, through her long ovipositor, or egg-laying tube. About two to six weeks later the eggs have developed into baby seahorses, ready to be born.

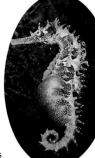

1 The male seahorse grasps a seaweed stem with his curly tail. The opening to the pouch has enlarged slightly, and the babies are moving around inside.

2 He bends his body backward and forward. The pouch opening widens and a baby seahorse shoots out. It rises to the surface and takes a gulp of air to fill its swim bladder (p. 8).

3 As the father continues to bend and stretch, more baby seahorses are born in batches of five or so. Each is less than half an inch long, and soon starts feeding on tiny water creatures. The father is very tired by the end of the birth session, which can last two days.

WEEDY HORSE

Australasia's leafy sea dragon is one of the largest seahorses, growing to more than 12 in (30 cm) in length. It is covered with fleshy flaps and weedlike trailers, making it extremely difficult to spot in its favorite haunt of shallow, seaweed-filled bays. It is often found cast ashore after storms because it is a weak swimmer and lacks the prehensile tail of other seahorses.

SPOT THE PIPEFISH

The pipefish's long, thin shape and banded green-brown color give it excellent camouflage among the wracks, eelgrasses, and other long, slim seaweeds around the shore. Like seahorses, pipefishes often swim and rest in an upright posture, looking a lot like strands of weed. Although it looks soft and vulnerable, this fish's body has a tough outer case that limits its twisting movements. The male keeps the eggs in a pouch formed by two long flaps of soft skin along his lower abdomen. After the babies hatch, they often dash back to the safety of the father's pouch when they sense danger.

TOGETHERNESS

Male and female pipefishes court by swimming upright past each other. Then the male rubs the female's abdomen with his snout several times. Eventually they intertwine and she deposits the eggs in his pouch. Unlike the male seahorse, the pipefish's brood pouch literally bursts to release the young.

Resting in an upright position, the pipefish is well hidden amongst the seaweeds

Pipefish

Small pectoral fin

Long, tubelike snout

Changing faces

THERE ARE ABOUT 520 species in the flatfish group – a group of fishes that live flat against the ocean floor. However, flatfishes are not born flat. When they hatch they look much like any other larval fish swimming upright near the sea surface. But within a few weeks, remarkable changes take place in their body's shape. The larval flatfish's body becomes very thin and flat. The eye on one side gradually moves over the top of the head to sit next to the eye on the opposite side. All this shifting leaves one side of the fish "blind" – this becomes the underside. The little fish sinks to the bottom, and the sea bed becomes its home. For the rest of its life, the adult flatfish lies on its blind side.

SOLE SEARCHING
The flatfish shown metamorphosing (changing) here is a European or common sole, which grows up to 24 in (60 cm) long. It is probably the most plentiful member of the sole family in European waters. This fish, also called a Dover sole, spends its days partly buried in sand or gravel.

1 THREE DAYS OLD
This side view of the baby sole, three days after hatching, shows a fairly normal-looking larval fish. The backbone is in its early stage of development, and a few pigment cells have formed on the otherwise transparent body.
Actual size: .14 in (3.5 mm)

Yolk sac still visible

Eye

2 FIVE DAYS OLD
The sole's left eye can be seen as a shadowy spot on the other side of the head. At this stage the larval flatfish still swims in the upper waters of the sea, where the eggs hatched, and lives off the nutrients in its yolk sac.
Actual size: .14 in (3.5 mm)

Vertebrae begin to form

3 EIGHT DAYS OLD
More pigment cells grow in the skin, and the skull, jaw bones, and backbone develop further. In a bony fish the shape of the skeleton forms first in cartilage, which gradually ossifies, or hardens into true bone.
Actual size: .15 in (3.8 mm)

Pigment cells

Backbone is further developed

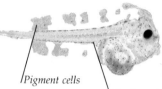

Skin pigment cells merge to form blotches of dark color

11 FORTY-FIVE DAYS
Nearly seven weeks after hatching, the sole looks like its parent in miniature. Skin pigment cells merge to form blotches of dark color. Now the sole will live on the bottom for the rest of its life. Of the half million or so eggs released by the female parent, very few reach this stage. Even fewer, perhaps only one or two, will grow into mature adults.
Actual size: .43 in (11 mm)

NEARLY A YEARLING
This sole, approaching its first birthday, shows its changeable skin coloration under a mosaic patterning of ctenoid (comb-edged) scales.

Skull has grown more quickly on the left

DISAPPEARING EYES
Young California blind gobies have small eyes and can see. But as they grow, the eyes disappear under the skin. This fish lives in dark crevices and shellfish tunnels near the shore.

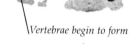

10 THIRTY-FIVE DAYS
Metamorphosis is almost complete. The skull has grown more quickly on the left, causing that side to enlarge and swing the left eye over to the right. By this age the young sole has drifted from the hatching ground into the coastal shallows.
Actual size: .39 in (.10 mm)

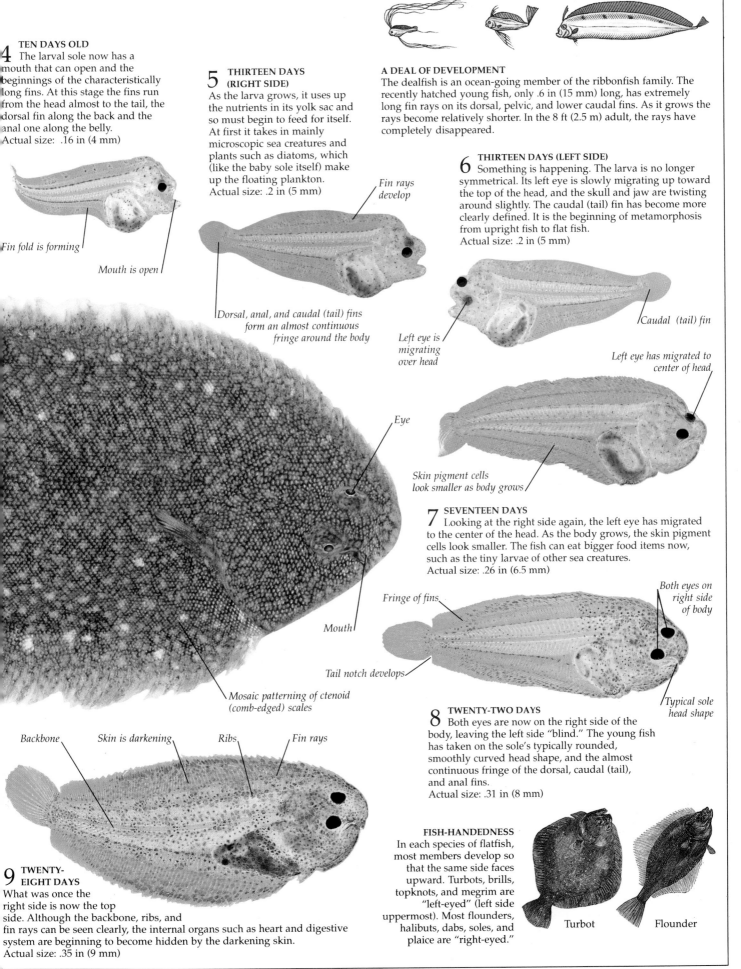

4 TEN DAYS OLD

The larval sole now has a mouth that can open and the beginnings of the characteristically long fins. At this stage the fins run from the head almost to the tail, the dorsal fin along the back and the anal one along the belly.
Actual size: .16 in (4 mm)

Fin fold is forming

Mouth is open

5 THIRTEEN DAYS (RIGHT SIDE)

As the larva grows, it uses up the nutrients in its yolk sac and so must begin to feed for itself. At first it takes in mainly microscopic sea creatures and plants such as diatoms, which (like the baby sole itself) make up the floating plankton.
Actual size: .2 in (5 mm)

Fin rays develop

Dorsal, anal, and caudal (tail) fins form an almost continuous fringe around the body

A DEAL OF DEVELOPMENT

The dealfish is an ocean-going member of the ribbonfish family. The recently hatched young fish, only .6 in (15 mm) long, has extremely long fin rays on its dorsal, pelvic, and lower caudal fins. As it grows the rays become relatively shorter. In the 8 ft (2.5 m) adult, the rays have completely disappeared.

6 THIRTEEN DAYS (LEFT SIDE)

Something is happening. The larva is no longer symmetrical. Its left eye is slowly migrating up toward the top of the head, and the skull and jaw are twisting around slightly. The caudal (tail) fin has become more clearly defined. It is the beginning of metamorphosis from upright fish to flat fish.
Actual size: .2 in (5 mm)

Left eye is migrating over head

Caudal (tail) fin

Left eye has migrated to center of head

Skin pigment cells look smaller as body grows

Eye

Mouth

Mosaic patterning of ctenoid (comb-edged) scales

7 SEVENTEEN DAYS

Looking at the right side again, the left eye has migrated to the center of the head. As the body grows, the skin pigment cells look smaller. The fish can eat bigger food items now, such as the tiny larvae of other sea creatures.
Actual size: .26 in (6.5 mm)

Fringe of fins

Tail notch develops

Both eyes on right side of body

Typical sole head shape

8 TWENTY-TWO DAYS

Both eyes are now on the right side of the body, leaving the left side "blind." The young fish has taken on the sole's typically rounded, smoothly curved head shape, and the almost continuous fringe of the dorsal, caudal (tail), and anal fins.
Actual size: .31 in (8 mm)

Backbone *Skin is darkening* *Ribs* *Fin rays*

9 TWENTY-EIGHT DAYS

What was once the right side is now the top side. Although the backbone, ribs, and fin rays can be seen clearly, the internal organs such as heart and digestive system are beginning to become hidden by the darkening skin.
Actual size: .35 in (9 mm)

FISH-HANDEDNESS

In each species of flatfish, most members develop so that the same side faces upward. Turbots, brills, topknots, and megrim are "left-eyed" (left side uppermost). Most flounders, halibuts, dabs, soles, and plaice are "right-eyed."

Turbot   Flounder

Continued on next page

Flat fishes

Like most flatfishes, the plaice lives on or near the sea bed, well camouflaged by its spotty coloration. It swims by flapping its entire body up and down in a wavelike motion. Then it stiffens and glides down to land on the bottom, where it swishes its fins to brush up mud, sand, or gravel. The particles settle back over the fish's body and partially cover it, breaking up its outline and making it even more difficult to see.

Blood vessels and zigzag blocks of muscle visible on underside of plaice

Left pectoral fin

WHITE SIDE DOWN
The plaice is a "right-eyed" flatfish – it keeps its blind left side flat against the sea bed. Since this side is not normally visible, the fish doesn't need to make and maintain skin pigment cells to color it. So the underside is usually a natural flesh-colored white or cream. However, some plaice also have pigmented undersides, a condition known as ambicoloration.

Lower gill cover

Pelvic fin

Upper gill cover

Eyes are on right side

PLAICE FACE
As this front view shows, flatfishes are not truly flat. The upper side is more rounded than the underside, which gives the fish a low humped shape. During metamorphosis, the plaice's mouth twists only slightly from its original position.

Small scales embedded in skin

Spotty coloration changes according to background

White underside is
not normally visible

Blood vessels
visible

Caudal fin (tail)

Eyes face upward
on lemon sole
skeleton

FLAT SKELETON

At first glance, this could be the skeleton of a
deep-bodied, disk-shaped fish that swam upright.
The hole at the front below the head is for the
heart and other main internal organs. But a closer
look at the head reveals two eyes facing right – or
rather upward. This is the skeleton of a lemon
sole, another type of flatfish. Compare it with the
cod skeleton on page 10. The backbone, ribs, and
fin rays all correspond, although their proportions
differ somewhat. Only the front of the lemon
sole's head is twisted. However, the lemon sole is
not actually a true sole, but is more closely related
to the dab and the plaice.

Spots from back
showing through
on underside

CHAMELEON FISH

As flatfishes evolved to their
present relatively inactive life on the
sea bed, they became easy meals for
predators. But some survived because they
had evolved the ability to change skin
pattern and color, to blend in with different
backgrounds. Blending camouflage still
protects flatfishes today, and also helps
them to remain unnoticed by their
own prey – until the last second.
Nerves and hormones control the
color changes. Each skin pigment
cell (chromatophore) has fine
branches into which it can spread
its pigment grains; this colors a
tiny area of skin around each cell. If
instead the grains are drawn tightly
into the center of the cell, the
background sea bed
color shows through.

Flounder

Turbot

Plaice

THE FLAT FAMILY

There are about 500 species of
flatfishes, and they all have one
thing in common – their flatness.
The flounder, about 20 in (50 cm)
long, can live in the sea or in fresh
water. The turbot, a left-eyed
flatfish, grows to 3 ft (1 m) and
eats mainly other fishes. The plaice
is smaller, usually around 20 in (50
cm). Soles live in shallow coastal
waters and hunt for food at night.
Dab larvae migrate to deeper
waters – up to 230 ft (70 m) –
before beginning metamorphosis.

Sole

Dab

The art of swimming

IF YOU CAN "SWIM LIKE A FISH" it means that you have mastered the art of swimming, something that comes naturally to fishes. They swim like snakes wriggle: by a series of S-shaped curves, or "waves," that travel along the body. Each wave begins with a small sideways motion of the head, but becomes bigger as it sweeps along the body, so that the tail moves much farther sideways. The body and tail push the surrounding water sideways and backward, and so propel the fish forward. Most fishes use their tails primarily to propel themselves forward, but some species "row" with their pectoral fins instead. Each S-shaped wave is produced by contractions of muscle blocks on either side of the backbone. Each muscle block, or myotome, contracts a split second after the one in front of it, pulling that side of the body around into a curve which forms the wave. In a steadily swimming dogfish there is about one complete wave each second.

TALE OF THE WHALE
The tail of a whale (a mammal) is horizontal, unlike the vertical tail (caudal fin) of a fish. A whale swims by arching its body up and down, rather than from side to side as a fish does. Whales such as the humpback can accelerate under water and hurl their 50 tons of bulk clear out of the water, and fall back with an enormous splash. This is called "breaching."

Second dorsal fin

Caudal fin (tail)

Spotty coloration

First dorsal fin

"S" FOR SWIMMING
In this sequence of photographs, which covers about one second of time, the S-shaped wave of movement passes along the body of the dogfish and is "thrown off" by the tail. To begin new waves the head swings slightly, first to one side and then the other. The equal, but opposite movements to the left and right cancel each other out, and the fish is propelled forward. Compared to species such as the eels, the dogfish does not have a very flexible body.

A new S-shaped wave begins as the lesser spotted dogfish swings its head slightly to the right

The "peak" of the wave has passed along the body to between the pectoral and pelvic fins

The peak has now traveled to the region of the pelvic and first dorsal fins

TOPSY-TURVY FISHES
Many fishes can turn on their sides and even roll right over. But a few can actually swim upside-down for long periods. One of these is the upside-down catfish, originally from the Congo region of Africa and now kept in tropical freshwater aquariums around the world. Its mouth is on the underside of the head, as in other catfishes. This is ideal for grubbing around on the bottom, but not for taking items from the surface. The upside-down catfish has solved the problem by turning right over, so that it can catch flies and other prey that have fallen onto the water's surface.

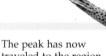

UPSIDE-DOWN SHADING
In upside-down catfishes, the normal countershading of dark back and light underside (p. 18) is lacking or even reversed, so the fish has a dark belly and a pale back. The aquarium upside-down catfish (left) is about 2 in (6 cm) long. The position of the lateral line when upside-down is shown in a related species (above).

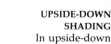

28

FIN-DRIVEN RAY

Although a ray can swish its tail from side to side, the tail itself is little more than a thin whip and so has hardly any pushing power. Most rays swim by waving the edges of their very wide pectoral fins and "flying" through the water. An S-shaped wave is again the basis of movement, although in this case it moves vertically (up and down) rather than horizontally (sideways). The wave begins just to the side of the head and passes along the pectorals to the pelvic region at the base of the tail.

REVERSIBLE EEL

The swimming sequence of an eel is similar to the dogfish (below). In this case, the whole long, thin body acts as a thruster, pushing the water alternately to one side and then the other – but always backward, as well. An eel can reverse the direction of the S-shaped wave so that it "flows" from tail to head – and so swims backward.

CURVE OF THE DOGFISH

Seen from above, the dogfish (a small shark) shows the subtle S-shaped body curve which initiates the fish's forward movement. As in most sharks, the pectoral and pelvic fins are not very flexible. They work mainly by tilting slightly, like the flaps and elevators of an aircraft wing, making the fish swim up or down, or bank and steer to one side.

Eye

Lesser spotted dogfish

Pelvic fin

Pectoral fin

As the peak
reaches the area between the two dorsal
fins, the tail begins its right thrust

This wave's peak
reaches the tail.
Meanwhile the snout
has begun another wave.

MOVING IN 3-D

A fish moves in three dimensions: forward and backward, left and right, and also up and down. The surfaces which control fine movements are the fins, including the caudal fin (tail). In order to change direction, the fin is tilted at an angle to the flow of water. The water presses on the fin, trying to straighten it. This exerts a force that turns the fish's body. A submarine is controlled in the same way, with a rudder at the rear to steer left or right, and horizontal hydroplanes to tilt the craft up or down.

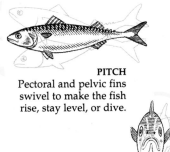

PITCH
Pectoral and pelvic fins swivel to make the fish rise, stay level, or dive.

ROLL
Dorsal fins (also pectoral and pelvics) make the fish roll on its own axis.

YAW
Moving to the left or right ("steering") using a combination of fin angles.

A rocket flying through air must stay stable in three dimensions, as a fish does when swimming through water

Tails and fins

Sailfish tail

A FISH USES ITS FINS not only to swim forward and turn, but to stop and stand still. Most fishes propel themselves forward using all of their fins, but especially the caudal or tail fin. Their pectoral, dorsal, and pelvic fins enable them to steer and stop. It is possible to guess a fish's way of life from the shape of its fins. A fish with slim, knifelike side fins and a narrow forked tail, as the tuna or sailfish have, is probably a fast cruiser. A fish with relatively large, broad side fins and a wide, square-ended tail is good at moving in and around rocks and reefs but is probably a slow swimmer.

SAIL TAIL
The sailfish (p.10) is one of the fastest of all fishes, traveling at speeds estimated at more than 60 mph (96 kph). The "lunate" or crescent-shaped tail, narrow yet deep, is typical of fishes that cruise at high speed. It has little flesh and few scales, and is made mostly of fin rays. The tail is only slightly flexible, but is incredibly strong, to transmit the enormous power of the body muscles through to the water.

Tail is crescent-shaped for speed

KINGFISH FINS
The kingfish's round body shape is not at all streamlined, but its long fins compensate and help it move fast through the water.

ON TIPTOE
Enormous pectoral fins and plenty of spiny fin rays make the tub gurnard an extremely prickly fish. The first three rays of each pectoral fin are separate, and move back and forth like spider's legs as the gurnard "tiptoes" along the sea bed.

Soft edge on sucker seals to host skin

Remora sucker

Plates in sucker tilt to create a vacuum

STUCK ON SHARKS
The remora has evolved a dorsal fin that acts as a powerful sucker. It often sticks to a blue shark, hitching a ride and feeding on the host shark's parasites and perhaps sharing in any leftovers.

Long upper lobe turns upward on fish

UNLIKELY TAIL
The butterflyfish tail is just barely divided into two lobes. This specimen caught in East Africa bore markings that resembled, presumably by chance, old Arabic writing which translates as "There is no God but Allah." Consequently, it fetched a hefty price at the fish market!

UNEQUAL LOBES
The sturgeon's uneven caudal fin is called a heterocercal tail – the fish's backbone extends upward into the upper lobe, and most of the rays that form the two lobes of the tail fin come from the backbone's underside. The rays from the upper side of the backbone form only the small topmost part of the tail. Many sharks also have this kind of uneven tail.

Fin rays

Sturgeon tail

Butterfly-fish tail

FUSED TAIL
In some species of armored catfishes, the upper and lower lobes of the tail fin are joined to form one large fin surface.

Notch on tail fin

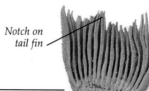

Armored catfish tail

FISH SHOULDER
The bases of the pectoral
fins are linked to the
body by the bones of
the shoulder girdle, which can be
compared to human shoulder joints.
This is the shoulder girdle of the
upside-down catfish, which sculls
along with its large fins (p. 28). The
fin spines can be locked rigidly upright.

*Fin rays are loaded
with poison in life*

*Rays of fin
fan out when
fish is in
flight*

ON THE WING
Flyingfishes leap from the water
and glide (rather than fly) on their
long pectoral fins. The fins fold
against the body when swimming,
but as the fish takes off, the rays are
opened out in a fanlike fashion to
make a "wing."

DEATH RAY
In life, the
long, slender fin rays of the
lionfish are loaded with
deadly poison (p. 55). The
rays are very colorful and
mostly separated, instead of
being joined by the usual
weblike fin membrane.

Flyingfishes in flight above
the water surface

Interlocking ring in back

Ring at base of spine

Fin spine

RAISING RAYS
In many catfishes, the first ray or
rays of the dorsal fin have evolved
into strong spines that can be raised
or lowered by a special joint consisting
of two interlocking rings. This is a spine joint from
a sea catfish.

*Dorsal spine
locked upright*

LOCKED UP
The front dorsal spine of the
triggerfish can be locked
upright by the second
"trigger" spine that slots
down behind it.

Trigger spine

OPEN EYED
With a sudden swish,
the eyed *Pteraclis* raises
its huge, expandable dorsal
and ventral fins. The fish
seems to become enormous and
the dark eyespot helps
to startle predators.

*Square end
of tail fin*

CUT-OFF CAUDAL
This parrotfish's broad,
square-ended caudal fin
shows that it is a slow
swimmer – usually grazing
coral reefs, capable of only an
occasional dash to safety.

TWO-LOBED CAT
Some armored catfishes have a
distinctly two-lobed caudal fin; each
lobe consists of
thickened fin
rays, making the
tail very strong but
not very flexible.

Overlapping lobes

Armored
catfish tail

Parrotfish tail

Fishes with legs

FINS LIKE OARS
Blennies have strong pectoral fins, which can be used as oars to "row" across bare rock when stranded out of water in their rocky shore habitat. This blenny is on the shore, probably on its way to a shallow pool.

Pᴇᴏᴘʟᴇ ᴜꜱᴜᴀʟʟʏ ᴘɪᴄᴛᴜʀᴇ ꜰɪꜱʜᴇꜱ swimming in water. But some kinds of fishes can actually "walk," using their fins as "legs," and even leave the water and breathe air for long periods of time. Mudskippers, for instance, "skip" across coastal mudflats and mangrove (tropical tree) swamps in Africa, Southeast Asia, and Australasia. They breathe by way of a kind of "aqualung," through water trapped inside their large gill chambers. The gurnard uses the spiny rays of its pectoral fins to creep delicately along the sea bottom (p. 30). Some African catfishes elbow their way across dry land much the way mudskippers do, looking a bit like combat soldiers crawling on their chests. Some fishes, such as climbing perches, can absorb oxygen directly from the air. They gulp it into their mouth and throat, where folds of skin or other special structures have a rich supply of blood vessels which pick up the oxygen. Climbing perches have even been found in trees.

LEGLESS FISH
The "fizzigiggious fish," a strange character in an Edward Lear nursery rhyme, always walked on stilts, because he had no legs!

Moist muddy surface

FISH ON STILTS

The curious tripod fish dwells in the dark depths 9,800 ft (3,000 m) below the sea's surface. Its two pelvic fins and the lower lobe of its tail fin extend into long stiff filaments. The fish props itself up on these, like stilts, and stands on the ocean bottom.

Tripod fish

Tripod fish can prop itself up on these long stiff filaments

FISHES WITH LUNGS

Fully equipped with lungs as well as gills, lungfishes can breathe out of water. These fishes have been in existence for 300 million years. The African lungfish (right) has burrowed into the mud at the bottom of a dried out swamp. After burrowing, it secretes mucus to form a cocoon which keeps in moisture. The fish breathes through a porous mud plug at the top of the burrow until the drought is over. The Australian lungfish (below) is literally in a family of its own. Although it rises to the surface to gulp in fresh air, it cannot hibernate to survive drought, and only abandons gill-breathing under very bad conditions.

African lungfish hibernating in mud burrow during a drought

Australian lungfish

A WALK IN THE MUD

In Southeast Asia, a muddy coastal swamp sweats in the tropical heat. Most water creatures are following the tide down the shore, or burying themselves in the safe dampness of the mud. But here and there, small wedge-shaped, pop-eyed creatures scurry across the moist surface, feeding on insects, attracting mates, and defending their territories. These mudskippers (below) can prop themselves up and skip quickly on their muscular pectoral fins, which look like stubby crutches. In addition to using its gill chambers as an aqualung when out of water, the mudskipper can absorb oxygen directly from the lining of its mouth and throat.

Mangrove trunks

A thick layer of clear skin protects bulging eyes

To keep eyes moist out of water, mudskippers can roll them back into the moist sockets

Short muscular pectoral fins look like stubby little legs out of water

Dorsal fin

Fishes feeding

THE BLOODSUCKER
The lamprey, one of the few jawless fishes, feeds by attaching itself to its prey with a sucker. It then scrapes with its teeth at its prey's flesh and sucks the blood.

"BIG FISHES EAT little fishes, and little fishes eat even smaller fishes . . . but what do these even smaller fishes eat?" This old question was soon solved when naturalists could look through a magnifying lens. The food chain in water, as on land, is based on plants. Most plants in the sea are microscopic and are called the phytoplankton. Microscopic animals, or zooplankton, eat these tiny floating plants; small creatures such as shrimps eat the plankton; and so the grand food web of life continues. The head of a fish gives many clues to its diet. Large, flat, crushing teeth indicate a diet of shellfish, corals, or tough plant matter; sharp, pointed teeth indicate a hunting lifestyle; and a wide, gaping mouth means the fish feeds by gulping.

SKEWERED FISH
The popular notion of a swordfish with an unfortunate victim impaled on its sword is shown in this fanciful engraving.

Elephant-trunk fish skull

Tiny jaws at end of "nose"

POKING ITS NOSE IN
The elephant-trunk fish from Africa has a long, curved "nose" with tiny jaws at the end. It pokes these between stones, into cracks, and down into the mud to find its food of small water creatures.

Pouting mouth for sucking in food

Porcupine fish skull

European bream skull

SURPRISING JAWS
The European John Dory has a surprise in store for unwary prey. Deep-bodied but extremely thin, this fish creeps up on smaller fishes and prawns, swimming head-on to make itself look inconspicuous. Then its great jaws suddenly lunge forward and engulf the prey.

John Dory skull

CHEWING THROAT
The common or European bream, a silvery-olive freshwater fish, has a "pouting" mouth which it uses to sift and churn through the mud, sucking up small bottom-dwelling worms, shellfish, and insect larvae. These are then ground up by pharyngeal or throat teeth.

Pharyngeal teeth of bream

PRICKLES NO PROBLEM
The porcupine fish is well known for its ability to puff itself up and erect its spines when threatened (p. 38). Its diet consists of hard-shelled mussels and other shellfish, corals lurking in their stony homes, and even sea urchins hiding beneath their own spines. In each jaw, the teeth are fused to form a hard-edged biting ridge at the front, with a flat crushing plate behind.

FRUIT AND NUT CASE
The pacu, from the Amazon region of Brazil, eats fruits and nuts which fall into the river. Its strong, crushing teeth are at the front of its mouth, for gathering and biting food.

Strong, crushing teeth

Prawn

Trumpetfish skull with long snout

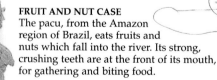

TRUMPETFISH TWEEZERS
A long, rigid "beak" extends between the trumpetfish's small mouth and eyes. The snout and the tiny teeth at the end are used like tweezers, to pull small aquatic animals out of their hiding places.

Hard-shelled mussels

Seed of *Pirhanea trifoliata* (the piranha tree)

Brazil nuts

BEWARE THE BARRACUDA

Fearsome predators found in warmer oceans, barracudas seize, maim, and tear up other fishes with their awesome array of spearlike teeth. The larger barracudas, which grow to nearly 10 ft (3 m) long, have been known to attack humans. However, many divers say the barracudas do not deserve their bad reputation. Although they may trail humans for some time, and they certainly look frightening enough, they rarely strike unless provoked.

Sharp, dagger-like teeth

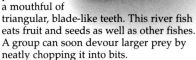

Sharp triangular teeth lock together for a clean bite

MOUTHFUL OF FANGS

The South American piranha has a mouthful of triangular, blade-like teeth. This river fish eats fruit and seeds as well as other fishes. A group can soon devour larger prey by neatly chopping it into bits.

STONY FACED

The wide, upward-facing mouth of the stonefish gulps in unwary prey as it lies on the sea bed, camouflaged by its remarkably rocklike appearance.

Wide mouth on top of head

Stonefish skull

SHARP NOSE

This is not a medieval sword, but the nose of the spectacular swordfish. The entire fish may be more than 13 ft (4 m) long; young swordfish have a relatively short bill (snout) which lengthens into the flattened sword as they mature. No one is sure exactly what the sword is used for. It may strike prey fishes, or impale them, or simply be a result of extreme streamlining, enabling the fish to swim faster.

CORAL CRUSHERS COMBINED

Coral reefs harbor an amazing variety of fishes, which have an equally amazing variety of feeding methods. The powerful, horny "beak" of the parrotfish is made of fused teeth. It scrapes the thin layer of algae and corals from rocks; the food is then ground to a powder by strong throat plates. The tapered snout of the forceps fish (p. 16) is ideal for inserting into nooks and crannies for small bits of food. Both the triggerfish and the leatherjacket's chisel-like teeth can bore holes in shells.

Horny beak

Parrotfish skull

Leatherjacket skull

Coral

Triggerfish skull

Forceps fish skull

Swordfish nose

SURFACE SKIMMER

The halfbeak, so named because the lower jaw is usually longer than the upper, skims the undersurface of the water, swallowing plankton and larval fishes.

CHAINSAW MASSACRE

This partly cutaway sawfish snout shows the "blades" of teeth in cartilage sockets. In fact this is a cartilaginous fish (p. 9), a close relative of the rays. Razor-sharp teeth on the saw can kill fishes. It is also used for probing into the sea bed to dig up food such as mollusks and crustaceans. The biggest sawfish are over 23 ft (7 m) long.

Sawfish snout

Sharp sawteeth in cartilage sockets

Food out of water

MOST FISHES FEED in their natural surroundings – water. Some, like trout, rise to the surface to snatch drowning flies and other food trapped at the surface or flying just above. But a few fishes are able to catch prey on land or in trees. The archerfishes are among the most expert. There are some five species of archerfishes, found in the tropical mangrove swamps of India and Australasia. Most of the time, the archerfish feeds on prey swimming or floating in the water. When enticed by hunger, however, this fish can squirt a jet of water droplets at insects and other creatures on leaves and stems above the surface. The surprise attack knocks the prey into the water, where the archerfish snaps it up.

Spider on leaf is the prey

Butterfly-fish

LEAPING BUTTERFLY
The West African butterflyfish swims close to the surface of grassy swamps and snaps up insects living at the surface. It can also leap out to catch a tasty morsel, at heights of over 6 ft (2 m) – some feat for a fish no longer than 4 in (10 cm).

Jet of water aimed at the spider

A DIRECT HIT
The archerfish swims slowly to a position just below its victim, looking up with its large eyes. Then it tilts its body almost vertical, rising so the tip of its snout is just at the surface, and lets fly with a volley of water drops. Shooting almost straight up makes it easier to aim at the target than shooting from the side. If the first volley of droplets misses, the fish can quickly adjust its aim and shoot again and again. Archerfishes begin to "spit" when very young, although they seem to do this largely at random and the jets only travel about 4 in (10 cm). As they get older, distance and aim improve. An experienced adult can score a direct hit on a victim more than 5 ft (1.5 m) above the water's surface.

THE ARCHER'S WATER-JET PUMP
When the archerfish is ready to "shoot," it snaps its gill covers shut, which compresses water in the gill chambers and mouth. The tongue presses upward against a groove in the roof of the mouth, turning the groove into a tube which produces a fast, narrow stream of water.

Groove in roof of mouth

Tongue acts like valve to keep water under pressure

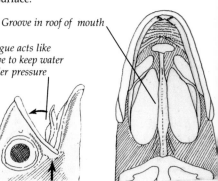

Side view of archerfish's mouth showing movement of tongue

Inside view of roof of archerfish's mouth

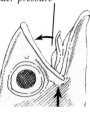

Spider on leaf is about to be snapped up by archerfish

LEAPING FOR ITS SUPPER
Archerfishes not only shoot at prey, they can also leap out of the water and knock the prey down. In an aquarium, they may jump up at food stuck to the side of the glass 12 in (30 cm) above the surface. They have also been seen leaping at and catching low-flying insects. However, it is not a success every time. Archerfishes jump or squirt at inedible objects such as marks on the aquarium glass or curious people leaning over to watch them. They often seem to shoot when they see a person blink, which is one in the eye for the observer! In the wild, these fishes prefer brackish (salty) waters in estuaries, but they will swim up rivers into fresh water.

AERIAL HUNTER
Deep in the Amazon rain forest lurks the arawana, a slim and agile fish with a cavernous, scooplike mouth. It feeds on water creatures such as shellfish and small crabs, and it may even eat small snakes. And, like the archerfish, the arawana can leap clear of the water in an attempt to catch an insect, small bird, or bat flying just above. These antics have earned it the local name of "water monkey."

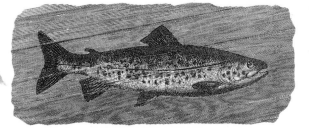

CRAFTY OLD TROUT
Trouts often rise to the surface to feed on drowning flies or other food trapped at the surface.

Scaring the enemy

LIGHT FOR LIFE
Many deep-sea fishes have luminous organs which can protect them from predators by either making them seem to "disappear," or by blinding the predator. This scaled dragonfish has luminous chin barbels.

IN THE UNDERWATER world, fishes are always ready to deal with an enemy – usually a predator on the prowl. A burst of speed is one way to foil the hunter. Size is another – very big fishes are sometimes too much of a mouth-ful, and very small ones can take refuge in cracks and crevices. Yet another tactic is camouflage (p. 50). Some fishes have evolved devious weapons to defend themselves against hungry hunters.The porcupine and pufferfishes, for example, can make themselves swell up and stick out their prickles or spines to discourage feeders. Triggerfishes have a spine on their back which can be locked erect by a bony projection of the smaller second spine. As a triggerfish struggles, its rigid spine can inflict great damage to a predator.

THE SURGEON'S SCALPEL
Surgeonfishes are colorful inhabitants of coral reefs throughout the tropical Pacific. The name comes from a sharp, bony, bladelike "lancet" on either side of the body, near the base of the tail. These blades cut flesh as cleanly as a surgeon's scalpel. In some species there is a row of small blades; in others the lancets lie folded in a groove when not in use, but can be flicked out quickly, like a switchblade, as the fish suddenly turns and thrashes its tail at an enemy. Surgeonfishes use their razors mainly for defense. Most of the time they graze among the coral and weeds, rowing along with their pectoral fins.

Surgeonfish

Pectoral fins

Tall, thin, deep-bodied shape

Long anal fin

Lancet blade

Lancet blade extended at right angles to the fish

*Spines lie flat along
body when porcupine
fish is at rest*

GOING UP

The porcupine fish is the hedgehog of the
fish world. Like a hedgehog, it can raise
its spines to make a prickly mouthful that
puts off potential predators. Unlike a
hedgehog, however, the porcupine
fish can also inflate its body like a
balloon, becoming far too large for
the average predator to swallow. There
are several species of porcupine fishes,
which live in mainly tropical seas.
The burrfishes, close relatives of
porcupine fishes, have spines that
are always semi-erect. Other
relatives are the pufferfishes, a few
of which live in fresh water.
They can also inflate their
bodies, but have shorter spines
than porcupine fishes. A
deflated or "relaxed" porcupine
fish (above) looks much like
many other fishes, although it
has very prominent eyes.
As soon as danger
approaches, this fish
quickly swallows water
and balloons to two or three
times its normal size. If a
porcupine fish is taken from
the water suddenly, it can take
in air instead of water to inflate in
the same way. When the
danger is past, the fish
slowly deflates.

*Spines swivel out to stand
at right angles to body
when porcupine fish is
inflated*

Pufferfish inflated to full
extent to scare enemy

Normal (deflated)
shape of pufferfish

*Pale underside
color is more
pronounced than
when deflated*

OUT OF PUFF

These before-and-after views of a
pufferfish show how the length of the fish
remains unchanged after puffing up.

Setting up house

Youngsters at the seaside: a black goby watches over its hatchlings

LIKE OTHER BABY animals, baby fishes develop from the eggs of the female, fertilized by the male. On land, mother and father must come together to mate. But for fishes, it is often enough for them to be near each other, since the water in which they live brings the eggs and sperm together. Thousands of fish species gather in the breeding season and spawn (lay and fertilize eggs) by simply shedding their roe (eggs) and milt (sperm) into the same patch of water. However, some species have courtship routines, usually where the male attracts the female with his bright breeding colors. The three-spined stickleback sets up a nest and guards it – another way to give eggs and young a better chance of survival.

NEST AT SEA
The male 15-spined or sea stickleback makes a nest, like its freshwater cousin. The fish puts small bits of seaweed in a large clump and then "ropes" it together with a sticky thread produced by the fish's kidneys.

RED AND BLUE BREEDERS
Every spring, in ponds, lakes, and rivers across the Northern Hemisphere, three-spined sticklebacks prepare to breed. Each male develops a splendid deep-red throat and chest, and bright blue eyes. He chases off other red-throated males and stakes out his territory – his own patch of water. Here he will build a nest, entice a female to lay eggs in it, fertilize them, guard them as they develop, and watch over the young as they hatch and grow.

Piece of water plant in stickleback's mouth for the nest

Bright blue eye

Red throat

1 COLLECTING THE MATERIALS
The male stickleback collects little pieces of water plants for the nest.

Beneath a small boulder is the ideal site on which to build a nest

Stickleback shovels gravel with his snout

2 DIGGING THE FOUNDATION
He pushes his snout into the stones and mud on the bottom, shoveling them aside to make a shallow hole. The male often builds the nest among water weeds or in the shelter of a small boulder.

3 A FIRM BASE
As the male begins to push pieces of plant into place, he taps and prods them firmly to make a secure base. The large fanlike pectoral fins are useful for the precise movements that this process requires.

Stickleback makes a firm base by prodding weeds into place with his snout

BLOWING BUBBLES FOR BABIES

The dwarf gourami, like many of its relatives, is a bubble-nest breeder. The male, dazzling in its breeding colors of shining turquoise and red stripes, lures the female to lay eggs. Then he fertilizes them and blows them into a mass of floating saliva-coated bubbles, where they begin their development.

4 CEMENT STAGE
As the pile of nest material grows, the male cements it together with a sticky "glue"– a secretion made by specialized parts of his kidneys. Gradually the nest grows, layer by layer.

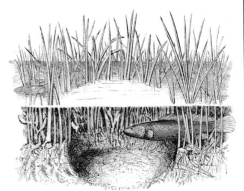

PATERNAL INSTINCT
The bowfin is a holostean fish (p. 9) from eastern North America. Each spring the male makes a rough nest of gravel, roots, and other pieces of plant, usually in a swampy part of his lake or river home. One or more females lay eggs in the nest; the male fertilizes the eggs and then guards them until the larvae hatch. The larvae attach themselves to the nest by glue-glands on their heads, feeding off their yolk sacs (p. 42) until they can swim freely.

5 ADDED VENTILATION
The collection of weeds and glue blocks fresh water from flowing through the nest. Fresh water is needed to bring oxygen to the eggs, and the fish uses his large fins to fan a current of water through the nest.

Fanlike pectoral fins create a current of water to aerate (bring oxygen to) the nest

Mouth agape in "yawn"

"Yawn" display

STICKLEBACK AT WORK
As the male selects his nest site and begins construction, he stops occasionally over the nest and performs quick motions like those above. Scientists believe that this is a "stay away" warning display to other fishes.

"S-bend" display

COMPLICATED COURTING
Like the male stickleback's, the male dragonet's colors get brighter during breeding and he displays his body and fins to the female in a courting dance. He attracts her with excited circling and other dancelike movements, then the two pair up and swim together, with their anal fins forming a channel through which eggs and sperm are released. After all this complicated activity, the parents swim off and leave the eggs to hatch on their own. He is about 12 in (30 cm) long; she is two-thirds this size and duller in color.

Male and female dragonet pair, ready to release eggs and sperm

Fish eggs

Genuine black caviar
(from beluga sturgeon)

Red caviar (from salmon) may be dyed black during processing

EGG ON TOAST
A few types of fish eggs, or roe, have become delicacies for the human palate in the form of caviar. People consume caviar partly for taste, and also because it is so rare. Unfortunately the fishing of mature females for caviar, even if they are put back afterward, is threatening the future of several species, especially the huge beluga sturgeon.

As A GROUP, FISHES SHOW almost the full range of breeding methods. Species such as cod and turbot release millions of tiny eggs, scattering them in the water to become fertilized and develop unaided. All but a handful of the millions will soon end up as food for other water creatures. On the other hand, the bullhead lays only one or two hundred eggs, and the male guards them fiercely as the embryos (babies) develop inside and hatch into fry. These are all oviparous species – that is, the eggs develop outside the body. Not all fishes lay eggs, however. Some species, such as sharks, are viviparous, like mammals. This means that the embryos grow inside the mother's body and she gives birth to fully formed young.

Round, yellowish clump of eggs

UNDER THE THUMB
In the springtime, "pincushions" of up to 250 round, yellowish eggs appear in stony shallow holes along the bottoms of rivers and lakes. These are egg masses of the female bullhead, or miller's thumb – so-called because its broad, flat head apparently resembles the wide thumb of a miller, who always tested flour and grain by rolling it between finger and thumb. The male bullhead guards and fans the eggs for up to a month as they hatch and the young begin to swim. However, any babies leaving later than one month are eaten by their father!

Broad, flat head gives miller's thumb its name

INSIDE THE EGG

These are the eggs of the three-spined stickleback (p. 40), seven days after fertilization, as seen under a low-power microscope. In life they are about .07 in (2 mm) across, and take from 5 to 12 days to hatch, depending on the temperature of the water. The developing embryo inside lives on nutrients from a bulbous, yellowish yolk sac until its organs form fully. When they hatch, the young, or fry, will be about .16 in (4 mm) long.

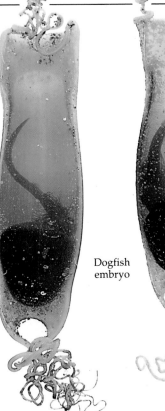

Dogfish embryo

Dogfish and her egg cases

BORN FROM A PURSE

The hard, horny "mermaid's purses" often found washed up on the beach are usually the dried-out, empty egg cases of dogfishes, skates, and rays. The male fertilizes the eggs within the female's body. The eggs begin to develop inside her body, then she lays them in pairs in their egg cases, attached to seaweeds by long, curly tendrils at each corner. The embryos grow inside the case and live on the yolk sac. They are about 4 in (10 cm) long when they wriggle out 6 to 9 months later.

Wide pectoral fins ideal for fanning and aerating the eggs

Chimaera egg case

CASE COLLECTION

Egg cases vary according to the type of fish that lays them. The chimaera (p. 20) produces a long tadpole-like case; the bottom-dwelling Port Jackson shark from Australia has a distinctive corkscrew-shaped case; while the spotted ray's case is more like the common "mermaid's purse."

Port Jackson shark egg case

Spotted ray egg case

Miller's thumb guarding clumps of eggs on rock

MUSSEL NURSERY

The bitterling chooses one of the most unusual places to lay her eggs. At spawning time in late spring, the female bitterling grows a long tube known as an ovipositor, through which she lays her eggs into the body cavity of the freshwater mussel, a shellfish living in lakes and slow rivers. The male bitterling releases his sperm nearby and the mussel sucks this in as it filter feeds. The male may then stand guard as the eggs develop and young hatch out to swim free from their shellfish nursery a month later.

Attentive parents

SOME SPECIES OF FISH seem to lack the maternal instinct. They release millions of eggs into the water and swim away, leaving the eggs at the mercy of nature (p. 42). But other species are remarkably attentive parents. Mouthbrooders, as the word suggests, refers to fishes like the cichlids that care for their eggs and young (fry) in their mouth and throat cavities. The female usually carries out this task. The male sea catfish does a similar job. Seahorse and pipefish fathers (p. 22) brood the eggs, and some species even protect their newborn young. Even sharks (p. 58), which normally attack any prey including their own kind, show a certain amount of parental consideration by not eating their babies! In some species the pups (baby sharks) are born in special "nursery grounds" in shallow water. The adult males rarely come to the area, and the females do not feed at this time. In this way the pups can get a safe start in life, instead of being food for their cannibal parents!

MOUTH POUCH
The Asian bonytongue, *Scleropages*, is an attentive parent that broods its eggs, and then the young, in a large pouchlike part of its lower jaw. The fish is a member of a small but ancient and partially air-breathing fish group, the bonytongues, which also includes the acrobatic arawana (p. 37).

MOUTHFUL OF EGGS
The red-finned cichlids of Africa's Lake Malawi are fussy parents. The male clears a shallow hole in a sandy or gravelly part of the lake bed. The female lays her eggs here. After the male fertilizes them, the female carefully takes the eggs into her mouth cavity for several weeks until they hatch.

Bright yellow bands of color give this mouthbrooder its name

Mouthbrooders

This term aptly describes a group of fishes that carry their eggs in their mouths. Even after hatching, the young fishes remain in the safety of their mother's "mouth nursery." Most mouthbrooders belong to the large cichlid family. The banded yellow mouthbrooder (right) is a cichlid, and lives in Africa's Lake Malawi.

OUT OF MOTHER'S MOUTH
The danger has passed. This banded yellow mouthbrooder "blows" her babies from her mouth, so that they can swim nearby and feed on tiny floating plants and animals. Now the mother can feed herself, too. When the fry are very young she holds them in her mouth most of the time. As they grow, the fry venture out more and more often, until they only return to her mouth at night or when danger threatens. Inside the mouth, the young are well protected and receive a constant stream of water carrying fresh supplies of oxygen for breathing.

Young cichlid being "blown" out of mother's mouth

Cichlids remain near their mother in case danger threatens

CLINGING ON

Many young creatures, including mammals, cling to their parents. Monkeys (right) cling to their mothers, but need to suckle on a teat for nourishment.

PARENT NIBBLERS

The fry of the common brown discus fish, from South America, "eat" their parents! In this unique form of parental care, the male and female keep their eggs clean and well-fanned with their fins for four days after laying, until they hatch. After about a week the adults start to feed the young with special secretions made by their skin. The babies gather around in a cloud to nibble at the parent's secretions, which are produced to nourish the young and are completely different from the usual fishy mucous coating. Parent-nibbling continues for about four weeks until the young start to swim away freely.

STIRRING UP MUD

At breeding time, the male African lungfish makes a deep pit in the swampy mud, where his partner (or sometimes more than one) lays her eggs. The father then fiercely protects the eggs and hatchlings for up to two months. He snaps at predators and drives them away – and at 6 ft (2 m) long, he is a menacing guard. He also swishes water through the nest by writhing his body, which keeps the young supplied with fresh water and oxygen.

A fierce defender of his babies - the African lungfish

Living in harmony

Yellow anemone

The little pilot fish
keeps sharks company
as they swim along

Many animals, including various fishes, can live in harmony together. Some fishes help others, and in the process help themselves. This type of relationship, which benefits all partners, is known as symbiosis. One amazing example involves cleaners – tiny fishes that swim trustingly right into the jaws of much bigger fishes. The cleaner's small mouth scrapes out parasites and bits of stale food. So the cleaner gets a meal while the big fish gets a "washing and brushing." Some fishes have even evolved specific relationships with a particular species. Clownfishes, damselfishes, and shepherdfishes shelter among poisonous sea anemone tentacles. The tentacles offer a safe refuge for the fish, while the anemone may absorb pieces of food dropped by its guests as they feed; the guests may even act as "bait" to draw other fishes into the anemone's deadly grasp. Various relationships between fishes and plants, other sea creatures, and other fishes provide both partners with protection, food, grooming, camouflage, and more. Indeed, the possibilities for living in harmony seem endless . . .

Bubble
anemone

LIFE IN A DEATH-TRAP
A large, jellyfish-like creature, the Portuguese man-of-war is a terror to sea life. Its stinging tentacles paralyze little fishes. But the little shepherdfish can swim unharmed among them. From the man-of-war it gains shelter and food, and in return it lures in fishes who are not resistant to the stings.

Clownfishes never stray far from the protection of the anemones

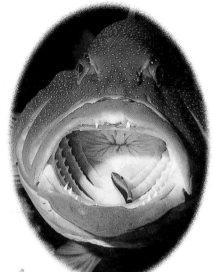

CLEANER AT WORK
A mutually beneficial partnership involves cleaner fishes, such as certain small wrasses, and their customers. The wrasses wait at a regular cleaning station, often at the same time each day, and are approached by larger individuals that require their services. The cleaner then picks fragments of food and parasites off the skin, fins, gills, and mouth – even right inside the throat. Here a tiny cleaner wrasse attends to a huge grouper in Australia's Great Barrier Reef.

Clown anemone

CLOWNING AROUND
On many tropical reefs, gaily colored clownfishes dart among a forest of tentacles. Yet the tentacles belong to a sea anemone, and bear venomous stings which would paralyze other small fishes in seconds. For years, it was a mystery how the clownfishes could live in their deadly refuge without being stung and dying. Recent research has shown that the clownfish has a thicker body covering of mucus than most fish. And the mucus does not contain the usual "fishy" substances which stimulate the anemone to sting. The clownfish may also become smeared with some of the anemone's mucus, which gives it even greater protection. However, clownfishes cannot dash into the arms of any old anemone. The poison from a different type, such as the fire anemone below, is too strong, and its sting could be the end of a beautiful relationship.

Fire anemone

The clownfishes avoid this anemone – even they are not immune to its fiery sting

Snakes of the sea

MORAY'S FORAY
Morays grow to 10 ft (3 m) long and live in warm coastal waters around the world. Many are brightly colored and are called "painted eels." Their fearsome reputation makes skin divers wary of them.

Eels, SLIMY AND WORMLIKE, resemble snakes more than fishes, and glide through the water the way snakes slither across land. They have been an important source of food since before Greek and Roman times, when it was considered a symbol of wealth to have a pond full of moray eels. They are long, tube-shaped fishes with apparently scaleless skin, no pelvic fins, and no spines in the remaining fins. There are about 600 species of true eels. These include freshwater eels, congers, morays, pike eels, and gulpers. Other fish groups have their own eel-shaped members, such as the electric eel of South America, which is more closely related to the knifefishes and catfishes. Perhaps the most intriguing thing about eels is their breeding pattern, which remained a mystery to people until the early 1900s (see right).

THE SERPENT'S TALE
For centuries, mariners have spun tales of great "sea serpents" terrifying their crews. Some sightings of these monsters may in fact be of large eels. But a more probable candidate might be the oarfish, a relative of the dealfish (p. 24), which grows to over 20 ft (6 m) long.

Pectoral fin

Gill opening

Yellow dorsal fin of ribbon eel

Pectoral fin

Skin is slimy and slippery

Front nostril

PELICAN EEL
The gulper eel lives in very deep waters and has a huge mouth and a tiny body.

Gulper eel

A TIGHT FIT
The brightly colored ribbon eel is a type of moray. Like its cousins, it lurks in cracks and caves, waiting for prey to pass nearby. It then seizes its victim with a fast, snakelike strike and a snap of its sharp-toothed jaws. The ribbon eel can coil itself backward into crevices that seem far too small for its long body.

MYSTERIOUS MIGRATION

For centuries, the European eel's breeding habits were a mystery. Adult fish lived in rivers and lakes, but each year, young eels (elvers) swam in from the sea in spring, and mature adults swam out to sea in the autumn. But eel eggs or larvae were never seen. Then in the 1920s, Danish zoologist Johannes Schmidt tracked the migrating eels to their breeding ground of the Sargasso Sea, in the western Atlantic. Scientists now believe that the adult eels spawn at great depths, and then die. The eggs hatch into leaflike larvae that live in the plankton. They drift toward Europe on the Gulf Stream current, arriving after two to three years. The larvae, now called leptocephali, do not resemble eels at all. Around Europe's coasts they change into elvers, or glass eels, enter the rivers, and begin to grow to adulthood.

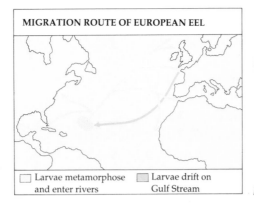

MIGRATION ROUTE OF EUROPEAN EEL

☐ Larvae metamorphose and enter rivers
▨ Larvae drift on Gulf Stream

European eels can glide through damp grass or slide through moist undergrowth to find a seaward river for migration

Dorsal fin

EEL BONES

A conger eel's skeleton reveals sharp backward-pointing teeth from which escape is almost impossible. An eel's long, tubular body and astonishing ability to slither through the water is made possible by the huge number of vertebrae in the backbone – more than 100 in many cases. There are no pelvic or caudal (tail) fins, and many species lack pectoral fins too. The dorsal and anal fins stretch right to the end and join to form a continuous fringe around the back of the tail.

STUNNING EEL

The electric eel (right) dwells in waters of the Amazon where there is little oxygen. Most of its body holds up to 6,000 electroplates – modified muscles arranged like tiny batteries. The eel can kill small fishes with 500-volt shocks. It uses much lower voltages to navigate through the murky water.

Sharp teeth

Rear nostril near eye

Great numbers of vertebrae in backbone for flexibility

Dorsal fin stretches right to the tail

Protruding lower jaw

CONGER'S GAPE

The fearsome conger lunges at anything edible, from an octopus to the groping fingers of a skin diver (which may look very similar). These eels spawn 13,000 ft (4,000 m) down in the mid-Atlantic.

Hiding places

THE "LANDSCAPE" of the underwater world varies just as it does on land, from cool green gardens of seaweeds, to the dazzling corals of tropical reefs, to deserts of sand or gravel, to rocky and jagged cavern-ridden cliffs. Like the familiar caves, treetrunk holes, and soft soil we see on land, each of these watery habitats offers opportunities for hiding places – which are useful for both predators and prey. Most of the hunted, like small wrasses, must feed out in the open; but at a second's notice they can dart out of harm's way, by digging themselves into loose sand or mud, or diving into a narrow cleft in the rocks. Hunters like the moray eel (p. 48) and the shore goby are content to lurk in cracks or caves, watching for unsuspecting victims to swim past.

Eyespots give the illusion of a big "face"

Wrasse is searching for a loose patch of gravel to dive into

SAFE IN THE SAND
The twinspot wrasse, from tropical reefs, has two large eyespots on its dorsal fin. If this huge "face" does not frighten the predator, the twinspot can dive into the coral sand or gravel and be out of sight within a few seconds. However, if the fish detects "danger" and reacts, but the danger turns out to be harmless, the fish may gradually stop its reaction. This "fading away" of behavior is known as habituation. Suppose a boulder became stuck in a gully and crashed back and forth in the waves. At first the wrasse might respond to the loud banging sounds by digging in each time. But gradually, if no danger actually appeared, it would come to ignore the noise. Which is just as well, since the boulder might bang for months.

2 **TESTING THE BED**
As the fish reaches the sea bed it swerves up to horizontal position and thrusts its sensitive snout and chest into the gravel. If this turns out to be only a shallow layer on top of solid rock and so no use for hiding, then the sooner the twinspot detects this, the better. Delay could mean death!

Wrasse's body is in a horizontal position and already throwing up gravel

1 **EMERGENCY!**
The twinspot detects a threatening sound, scent, or the sight of a potential predator. At once it tilts its head down and, as it dives, searches out a bare patch of gravel for refuge.

LOCKED FILE

The first spine of the filefish's dorsal fin has many tiny notches, and looks like a miniature version of a file (a ridged tool used for smoothing surfaces). However, its name originally came from the tiny spines on its scales, which give them a very rough texture, too. When in trouble, the filefish can swim into a crevice and lock its dorsal spine upright, as does its relative the triggerfish (p. 31). It is then wedged in and almost impossible to remove.

VANISHING GARDEN

Garden eels, from the Caribbean, live in large groups in warm, shallow tropical waters. Each eel has its own burrow, regularly spaced from its neighbors. With its rear end "rooted" in the sea bed, it snaps at small floating plants and animals that pass by. It has very small fins but can wriggle forward and backward with surprising speed. Garden eels are named for their resemblance to a well-kept garden, waving gently in the "wind" of water currents. When disturbed, they rapidly slide backward into their burrows and the entire "garden" disappears.

BOTTLED UP

This goby, a common shore fish, has taken refuge in the neck of a bottle. Fishes tend to treat man-made items with suspicion at first, but soon investigate their food value. As weeds and creatures slowly encrust the bottle, its artificial nature is obscured and it becomes just another useful "cave," for small fishes hiding from big ones, or for hunters waiting to ambush prey.

3 DIGGING IN Throwing its body into S-shaped curves, digging down in a diagonal direction, the twinspot "swims" head first into the loose gravel and stones. Its fins and tail fling the gravel upward out of the way.

Loose gravel flung upward by wrasse's activity

Body is in an S-shaped curve, to burrow more efficiently

4 OUT OF SIGHT, OUT OF MIND Within a few seconds, the fish is settled into the surface layer of pebbles, and the falling gravel rains back down to add to its covering. Here the twinspot stays until it senses that things are back to normal above. In fact many species of wrasse, especially around the Pacific coral islands, bury themselves in the gravel each night and "sleep" there. Others lie on their sides in caves and crevices. While the wrasses rest, the "night shift" of fishes take over and come out to feed and hunt on the reef.

Part of wrasse's body still visible in this photograph (but invisible to predators!)

Life on the move

WAITING WITH THE NETS
The great tuna schools have dwindled in numbers today, mainly because of overfishing. Their yearly routine of entering the Mediterranean sea in early summer makes them a predictable catch.

MANY KINDS OF FISHES SWIM TOGETHER in large groups called schools, or in looser collections called aggregates. Often, schooling is associated with feeding behavior – fishes, such as herring, follow each other in search of plankton-filled waters. Some species collect in great numbers in the breeding season. Protection from predators through "safety in numbers" is another way fishes benefit from swimming in schools, especially young fishes and smaller species. As a predator approaches a school, it is overcome by the bewildering numbers and activity, and is unable to pick out one individual prey. Small fishes in a dense school, moving in total unison, may discourage a predator by appearing as a single, much bigger creature. How do fishes achieve such harmony of movement? Visual markers play a big part – many schooling species have distinct bars or spots on their bodies, fins, and tails. The vibration-detecting lateral line (p. 7) also provides information about neighbors' movements.

Darker back for countershading (p. 18)

Lateral line runs low on body and can detect movements of other members of the school

SCHOOL AS A WHOLE
Common dace of Europe (also called dares or darts) often swim in large schools, especially when young. The fishes in the school dart and twist and turn in formation, moving together as if with one mind. In summer they swim just below the surface, often staying in the shade of a tree, and rising to the surface to catch flies and other insects. The dace lives in fairly fast, clear, gravelly rivers. Yearlings are about 3 in (7 cm) long; adult dace reach 10 in (25 cm).

Dashing habits of this fish give it the nickname of dart

The Atlantic herring, which grows to 16 in (40 cm) long

TOO EASY TO CATCH
Herring congregate in vast numbers and so are easy to net. In the days of sailboat fishing (above), catches were relatively constant. But since the 1950s and the advent of modern boats with school-locating radar and gigantic nets, herring numbers have declined – a clear example of overfishing.

A LINK IN THE FOOD CHAIN
A huge group of Pacific herring move through the clear waters of Baja California, off the Mexican coast. Such density of numbers suits the fishing industry's seine nets and otter trawls. Herring are also a vital link in the natural food chains of the sea, as prey of many larger fishes and seabirds.

SPOILT FOR CHOICE?
Yellowtail snappers of the western Atlantic hunt around reefs and rocks or smaller fishes and shellfish. This one is trying to feed on a dense school of small herring-like fish. The school darts back and forth with confusing speed. The snapper may become so confused that, despite the number of tasty tidbits before ts eyes, it ends up being unable to single out one to snap at.

Schools mill around in seeming confusion when they are changing direction

Eyes can look up and down

White underside

Silvery side

Poisonous fishes

MORE THAN 50 KINDS of poisonous fishes swim in the world's waters. Every year, people become severely ill or even die from the poison (also called venom or toxin) of stingrays, weevers, stonefishes, lionfishes, and other species. But these fishes did not evolve their venom in order to threaten humans. They use it mainly as a defense against larger predators such as big flatfishes and rays. Some unpleasant effects of fish poisoning on humans include numbness, paralysis, difficulty in breathing, uncontrolled bleeding, and blood poisoning.

The stargazer has poison spines above its pectoral fins

Thin, whippy tail

Delicate patterned tail

Three venomous anal spines

Stinger is a "dagger" of bone set into tail

Dinner or death?

Some fishes have flesh that, when eaten, is poisonous to humans. Certain types of pufferfishes are especially toxic. But the poison, tetrodotoxin, is confined to specific body parts of the fish. The flesh or muscle itself is said to be relatively safe and quite tasty. In Japan pufferfish (also called glovefish) is served in restaurants as the delicacy "fugu"; specially trained chefs prepare and cook the catch. Even so, despite various safeguards, people become severely ill and even die from eating fugu that has been prepared incorrectly.

Dead pufferfish awaiting preparation

THE RAY'S STING
The venom of a stingray's stinger comes from the shiny white tissue running along the two grooves under the spine. In European species the spine is about 5 in (12 cm) long. In larger tropical species it may reach lengths of 16 in (40 cm).

STING IN THE TAIL
More than 100 species of stingrays lurk in coastal shallows around the world. Some grow very large, with a "wingspan" of more than 10 ft (3 m), and weigh well over 661 lb (300 kg). They tend to hide in the bottom sand and sediment or glide along slowly as they search for shellfish and fishes to crack and crush with their rows of blunt teeth. When faced with trouble, these rays bring their stinger into play. The stinger is a spine-shaped, iron-hard "dagger" of bone set into the tail near its base. Some stingrays have two and even three stingers. The thin, whippy tail is of little use for swimming, but it is excellent as a stinging weapon. When threatened, the ray lashes its tail back and forth or arches it over its head, slashing and stabbing its stinger into the enemy. The stinger also has sharp, serrated edges that can inflict jagged cuts. And the poison acts quickly on humans, bringing on pain and swelling and causing problems with breathing and heartbeat. In severe cases, death can follow.

A pufferfish in pieces and ready for preparation. A sharp eye is needed to identify the poisonous organs.

Eating fugu: compliments to the chef - if you're still alive afterward!

*Thirteen
venomous
dorsal spines*

DEADLY BEAUTY
Lionfish, scorpionfish, zebrafish, dragonfish, turkeyfish,
firefish – call it what you will, this colorful and gaudy
creature is one of the most poisonous in the sea. Glands in
the spiny rays of its decorative, lacy fins make a powerful
venom that can cripple a predator and even kill a human.
The lionfish grows up to 16 in (40 cm) long and inhabits
shallow waters around reefs and rocks, in warm regions
from the Red Sea across the Indian Ocean to Australia and
the Pacific. Its graceful fins and bright-colored stripes warn
that this fish is not to be tampered with. For much of the
time it swims along, fins waving slowly, ignoring
predators. However, its lazy manner is deceptive. If the
lionfish spots a small fish or shellfish that looks like a tasty
meal, it can dart forward and strike with lightning speed.

STONY FACED
The stonefish is also a member of the scorpionfish
family. But unlike its colorful cousin the lionfish, it
has a warty, blotched body that blends perfectly
with the stony sea bed. Weeds and anemones
growing on its skin help to camouflage it. When
threatened, the fish raises the spines along its back.
Stonefish spines can inject the most potent of all
fish venoms, even through the soles of sandals. A
sting can maim, or even kill.

Eye

*Two venomous
pectoral spines*

Lionfish spine

Venom gland

Sheath

IN THE GROOVE
Each lionfish spine
bears a venom gland,
which lies in a long central
groove. The entire spine is also
covered with
glandular tissue.

Spiny fin ray

Base of ray

*Eye of
stingray*

Serrated edge

*Stinger contains
venom made
in shiny
white tissue*

*Large
pectoral
fin*

BE WARY OF THE WEEVER
The lesser weever (viperfish) lies partly buried in
sand, waiting for some food – small shellfish, crabs,
and other fish – to wander by. If attacked (or
stepped upon unwittingly) venom will flow from
glands at the bases of its erected, grooved spines on
the gill covers and first dorsal fin.

All about rays

The sawfish, a member of the ray group, uses its sawlike snout to protect itself.

R̶AYS ARE THE strange and graceful cousins of sharks, and belong to a group comprised of about 300 species, including skates and sawfishes. Because of their shape they are often confused with flatfishes – but there are several basic differences. Rays, like sharks, have skeletons made of cartilage – they lack the true bony skeleton of the flatfishes. And whereas flatfishes lie on their sides, rays are flat from top to bottom and lie belly down. This could pose problems in breathing, since gills on the underside could become clogged by sea bed mud. But rays have evolved a circular opening just behind each eye, called a spiracle, through which clean water flows into the gill chambers. Most rays stay on or near the sea bed and feed on fishes, shellfish, worms and other bottom-dwellers, which they grind up with their flat teeth.

Large, movable eye (rays have good eyesight)

Snout is sensitive to touch as the ray noses in sea bed mud

Spiracle – entrance for water to the gills as the ray lies on the bottom

Fin rays (struts) completely covered by flesh and skin, unlike bony fishes

Main row of bucklers, or thorns, along backbone

Back is color-camouflaged to conceal ray on sand, gravel, rocks, pebbles, and mud

Back view of female thornback ray

THORNBACK'S BACK
The thornback ray, also called the roker, is closely related and similar in appearance to the larger common skate. Thornbacks grow to about 3 ft (1 m); in length; skates grow to nearer 6.5 ft (2 m). This common species of ray is well camouflaged when lying on pebbly mud or sand. It rarely strays to waters deeper than 164 ft (50 m), and during the summer breeding season adults stay in shallower water. Young thornbacks feed on small fishes and shrimps. As they mature, they also begin to eat larger shrimps, crabs, and other shellfish, as well as flatfishes, sprats, and sand eels.

Dorsal fin

Bucklers along back

Thornback ray in resting pose

RAY AT REST
The aptly named thornback lies in its resting pose, showing off its main row of protective rosebush-like thorns, called bucklers. These are projections of the backbone along its back and tail. There are also spines on the sides of the tail, and two small dorsal fins toward its end. It holds its body slightly arched, which allows a free flow of water through the gill slits on the underside.

NO BONES ABOUT RAYS
Being a cartilaginous fish, the thornback has a skeleton of cartilage, not bone. The strutlike pectoral fin rays are expanded like a fan to form the flexible framework for the "wings" (compare with the fossil ray on page 11).

Nostril is opening to olfactory (smell) organ and is guarded by a flap (rays hunt largely by scent)

Horny mouth adapted for grasping shellfish and other bottom-living creatures

Five gill slits, one for each gill arch inside the gill chamber

Greatly expanded pectoral fins are joined to head to give typical diamond-shaped ray outline

A GIANT AMONG RAYS

The Atlantic manta or "devilfish" is the largest living ray, weighing in at well over 2 tons and having a wingspan exceeding 20 ft (6 m). It has a long, thin tail and lobed "scoops" (adapted from the front parts of the pectoral fins) on the front of the head to channel food into the great mouth. Despite their overwhelming size, mantas have small teeth and are gentle filter feeders, cruising the upper waters of warm oceans and consuming plankton, small fishes, and shellfish. They can also leap up to 5 ft (1.5 m) from the water. Their name comes from the Spanish for "blanket" and refers to the wide, cloaklike pectoral fins.

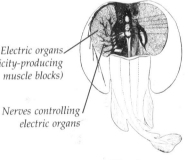

Electric organs (electricity-producing muscle blocks)

Nerves controlling electric organs

Electric ray sectioned to show electric organs

Spines on underside

Ray swims by up-and-down waving motion of its pectoral fins, "flying" through the water

Underside of female thornback ray

Small pelvic fins

WHAT A FACE!

Like the flatfishes, the ray does not need to have a colored underside, since it is usually on the sea bed and so is rarely seen. The nostrils and mouth form a curiously cheerful human-looking "face," and the cartilaginous fin struts are visible through the pale skin.

Atlantic torpedo or electric ray

SHOCKING RAY

Like several other fish groups, rays have their high-powered electricity-generating members. There are about 35 species of electric rays. One is the Atlantic torpedo or electric ray. It grows to more than 5 ft (1.5 m) in length. Like most rays, it lies lazily on the sea bed for much of the time, but occasionally stirs itself to feed. The torpedo preys on small fishes and shellfish. As the ray swoops, it wraps its pectoral fins around the victim and delivers shocks of over 200 volts from specialized muscle blocks on either side of its head.

The great warriors of the sea

Face to face with a fearsome fish foe: the dangerous end of a blue shark showing its mouthful of teeth

A TRIANGULAR FIN breaking the surface of an otherwise calm sea is something that strikes dread into the hearts of swimmers. Beneath the fin is the creature people love to hate, a fish whose predatory menace and mastery of the sea has made it infamous – the shark. Many sharks are powerful and efficient killing machines. They detect a likely prey with their finely tuned senses (including eyesight, smell, and electricity-detecting organs around the nose), then charge at sudden speed, and bite with bone-crunching power. Yet not all sharks are sleek, ferocious, and streamlined. The wobbegongs or carpet sharks of the Eastern Pacific and Australia are slow movers. They eat bottom-dwelling shellfish and rarely attack people unless severely provoked. Their round, flattish bodies are mottled with yellows, oranges, and browns, which help camouflage them as they lie among the rocks and weeds of the sea bed.

Thresher has a short, blunt snout

Large eyes for hunting by vision (threshers have better eyesight than most sharks)

Nostrils for hunting by scent

Small triangular teeth for grabbing prey

A shark's gill slits are separated and not covered by an operculum

THE PRIMITIVE HUNTER
Sharks are often called "primitive" creatures. This means that they appeared quite early in the evolution of the fish group, and they have survived largely unchanged, at least on the outside, for millions of years. However, in this sense, "primitive" does not imply that sharks are now out of date. Theirs was a highly successful design millions of years ago, and only slight changes have occurred since. An early type of shark was the 6 ft (2 m) long *Cladoselache*, which terrorized the seas 350 million years ago. The frilled shark, a "living leftover," seems to have become "stuck" at an early stage of shark evolution. It looks more like species of *Cladoselache's* time than a modern shark.

Cladoselache, from 350 million years ago

Frilled shark, a rare living deep-water species

THRASHING THRESHER
The thresher's remarkable tail (which is so long that it extends to page 61) accounts for this shark's various common names: fox shark, whiptail, thrasher, swiveltail, and swingle tail. The tail is used as a "thrash." The shark circles a school of smaller fishes, such as mackerel, pilchard, or herring, and sweeps them into a tight group by whipping the water with its tail. It then charges through the school open-mouthed, and snaps up dazed victims. Some people claim that the thresher can stun a fish with one blow of its tail, and flick it into its mouth with the next. The thresher is certainly an enthusiastic feeder – one specimen caught had a stomach bulging with 25 mackerel. Threshers live in warmer coastal waters in the Atlantic and eastern Pacific, although in summer they stray to cooler seas off northern Europe and New England. The thresher grows to 20 ft (6 m) long but reaches a mere 1000 lb (450 kg) in weight, since its tapering tail makes up half the overall length.

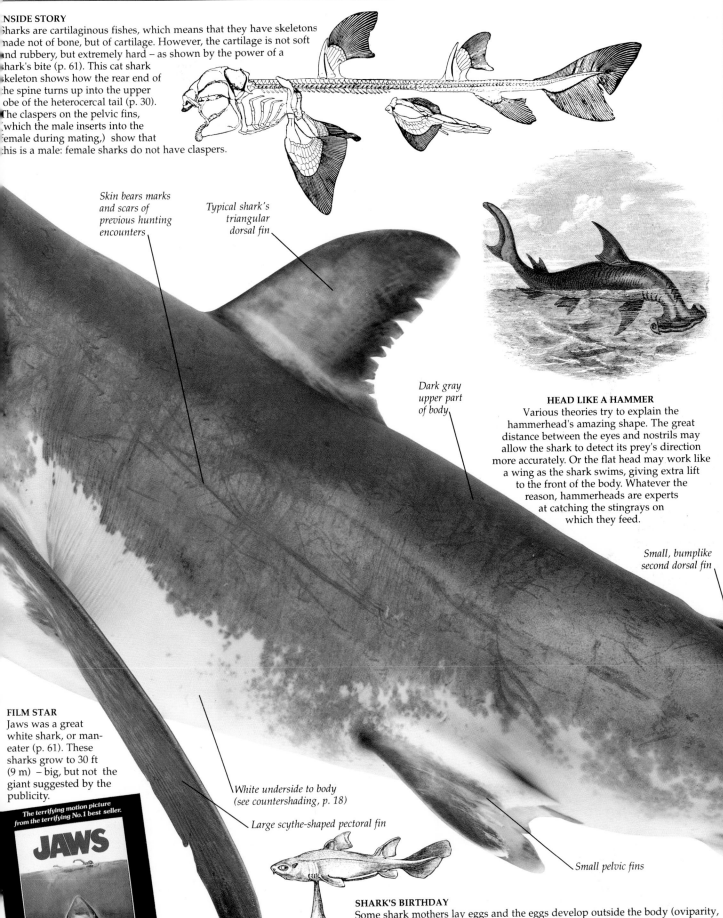

INSIDE STORY

Sharks are cartilaginous fishes, which means that they have skeletons made not of bone, but of cartilage. However, the cartilage is not soft and rubbery, but extremely hard – as shown by the power of a shark's bite (p. 61). This cat shark skeleton shows how the rear end of the spine turns up into the upper lobe of the heterocercal tail (p. 30). The claspers on the pelvic fins, which the male inserts into the female during mating,) show that this is a male: female sharks do not have claspers.

Skin bears marks
and scars of
previous hunting
encounters

Typical shark's
triangular
dorsal fin

Dark gray
upper part
of body

HEAD LIKE A HAMMER
Various theories try to explain the hammerhead's amazing shape. The great distance between the eyes and nostrils may allow the shark to detect its prey's direction more accurately. Or the flat head may work like a wing as the shark swims, giving extra lift to the front of the body. Whatever the reason, hammerheads are experts at catching the stingrays on which they feed.

Small, bumplike
second dorsal fin

FILM STAR
Jaws was a great white shark, or man-eater (p. 61). These sharks grow to 30 ft (9 m) – big, but not the giant suggested by the publicity.

The terrifying motion picture
from the terrifying No.1 best seller.

JAWS

ROY
SCHEIDER   ROBERT
SHAW   RICHARD
DREYFUSS

White underside to body
(see countershading, p. 18)

Large scythe-shaped pectoral fin

Small pelvic fins

SHARK'S BIRTHDAY
Some shark mothers lay eggs and the eggs develop outside the body (oviparity, p. 42). Others have eggs which develop and hatch inside their body, and the embryos feed off the yolk sacs (ovoviviparity). Some young sharks retain the yolk sac for a while after birth. Yet others nourish their young directly from their own blood supply, and give birth to fully formed young (viviparity).

Continued on next page

The warrior's weapons

The word "shark" seems to be unavoidably linked with "teeth." And sharks are certainly well supplied with them; in fact, sharks never stop growing new teeth. In most species the teeth are triangular or pointed, with sharp tips and serrated edges – a sure sign of a hunter. In a typical shark attack, if the prey is too big to eat in one gulp, the shark will clamp its teeth on the victim's body and shake its head from side-to-side, "sawing" off a mouth-sized lump.

LION-EATING TIGER
The wide-open mouth of a tiger shark displays rows of razor-sharp teeth in the upper and lower jaws. This species grows to 20 ft (6 m) in length and weighs the same as 15-20 adult humans. As the shark attacks, its jaws swing forward and outward, its snout turns up and out of the way, and its eyes roll inward in their sockets: all this helps the creature to get a clean snap at the prey. Tiger sharks eat whatever they can, from sea lions to squid, turtles, and other sharks.

Tiger on the prowl: in warm seas worldwide, the tiger shark hunts in as little as 3 ft (1 m) of water

HUNTING DOG
The lesser spotted dogfish is one of the smallest members of the shark family (p. 28). It has many small, sharply pointed teeth. This species hunts mostly by smell and feeds on or near the sea bed, eating worms, prawns, crabs, shellfish, and other bottom-dwellers. It is the most common shark in European waters, and is harmless to humans.

DREDGE AND CRUSH
Named after the busy harbor at Sydney, Australia, the inoffensive Port Jackson shark reaches about 6 ft (2 m) in length. It is not one of the active, sharp-toothed, torpedo-shaped predatory sharks. Instead, it dredges up shellfish, starfish, crabs, and other bottom-living animals from the sand and mud, and grinds them up with its broad, flat, crushing teeth.

Port Jackson shark

Razor-sharp teeth in upper jaw

Rows of tiny pointed teeth

Rows of flat, crushing teeth

Jaw joint

Jaw joint

Upper jaw cartilage (palatoquadrate)

Jaw joint

Lower jaw cartilage (mandibular)

Replacement teeth in lower jaw, waiting to be used

Functional teeth in lower jaw

Small lower lobe of thresher's tail

60

BIGGEST HAS THE SMALLEST
The world's biggest shark (and biggest of all fishes, p. 6) has some of the smallest teeth. Whale sharks have rows of "teeth" (modified denticles) in their mouth, along their gills, and in their throat and gullet. These act as a sieve, filtering small floating creatures from the water, as the shark cruises along slowly at about human walking speed.

Very long upper lobe of thresher's tail

Rows of whale shark teeth

Small teeth made from modified denticles (placoid scales, p. 14)

Basking shark

Lower jaw cartilage from basking shark

BASKER'S TEETH
A basking shark (the second-largest of all fishes) has many small teeth, but these are probably evolutionary leftovers. This huge creature, 30 ft (9 m) long, feeds by filtering the water with its gill rakers (p. 9).

THRESHER'S THRASH
The thresher's tail is extremely muscular, tough, and strong, like a thick leather strap, and can be flexed (bent) at will. A trapped thresher can do immense damage to the nets and other captive fishes as its tail (caudal fin) whips back and forth.

Fossil shark tooth is shown at less than actual size

WHITE DEATH
The great white is the most feared of all shark species. Experiments with a "bite-meter" show that a big shark can exert a force of 132 lb (60 kg) through just one tooth! The total biting pressure is many tons. Above is the skeleton of the jaws, which are slung loosely beneath the snout and the rest of the skull.

FOSSIL HUNTER
Prehistoric sharks, whose skeletons are made of cartilage, are preserved less often as fossils than are fishes with bony skeletons. However, the shark's extremely hard teeth have fossilized well. This great white shark fossil tooth is in fact as big as a human hand, which indicates that predatory white sharks such as *Procarcharodon* (of 20 million years ago) grew to almost 43 ft (13 m) in length!

TOOTHY JAILERS
Some prisons and captive colonies, such as Devil's Island off northeastern South America, were located on islands in shark-infested waters. The sharks made short work of convicts who attempted to escape.

A living legend: the fearsome great white shark looms out of the water

Exposed teeth ready for use

NEW TEETH
A shark continuously grows new teeth at the backs of its jaws. These gradually move forward, as if on a conveyor belt, until they reach the front of the mouth, where they swing outward ready for use. As the working teeth wear away or break off, new ones from behind take their place. These are the distinctive spearlike teeth of a mako (blue pointer), an extremely fast and ferocious species.

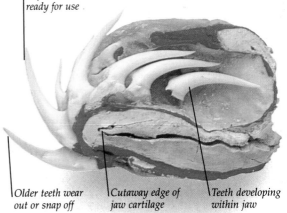

Older teeth wear out or snap off *Cutaway edge of jaw cartilage* *Teeth developing within jaw*

Studying fishes

IN LABORATORIES and scientific stations around the world, from the frozen Arctic to the steaming tropics, fishes are being studied by ichthyologists, or fish specialists (*ichthys* is Greek for fish). It is more than simple curiosity. Many of the world's peoples rely on fishes for food, especially for the protein part of their diet. Fish populations are constantly monitored, to determine whether overfished species are regaining their numbers, and to identify new stocks which could find their way into the fishing boat's nets. Most fishes are sensitive to small quantities of strange chemicals in the water, and their illness or disappearance from rivers, lakes, and seas shows that the waters are polluted. Healthy waters mean healthy fishes: they have twice as much of the earth to swim in than we have to walk on, and they ultimately reflect the health of our planet.

DARWIN'S FISHES
During his voyage around the world in HMS *Beagle*, in the 1830s, the eminent naturalist Charles Darwin collected and studied many fish species. A sea bass from Chile is shown ready for study at his desk (left). In his notes, he described a porcupine fish that had been swallowed by a shark but had then apparently eaten its way out through the shark's side: "Who would ever have imagined that a little soft fish could have destroyed the great and savage shark?"

Flexible spotlight for studying specimens under the microscope

Angled seeker or probe for parting blocks of tissue and various organs

Needle or ligament scalpel for cutting nerves

Fine scalpel for cutting muscles and vessels

TOOLS FOR THE JOB
Various specialized instruments are needed to examine the internal structure of a fish's body. The bones, muscles, and ligaments are tough and strong, and it requires great skill and care to expose the organs without damaging them.

SEE-THROUGH STAINING
Fish bodies are preserved and prepared using various chemicals, depending on what is to be studied. In the alizarin technique, the creature's flesh and soft organs are turned to a transparent jelly, and the harder parts such as bones and fin rays are stained deep pink by the alizarin dye (obtained originally from the madder plant of India). The complete skeleton can then be studied under the microscope, revealing the shapes and proportions of the various bones.

Bone chisel for cutting through tough outer scutes and thick bone

Scalpel for cutting through outer skin and scales

FISH GALLERY
Reference books and catalogues help to identify a new or unfamiliar specimen. Photographs cannot lie, but often a good painting is better at conveying the essential features of a species.

Fine forceps or tweezers for lifting out various vessels and small organs for study

Syringe and hypodermic needle for injecting preservatives into fish

X-RAY FISH
The bones and cartilages of fishes, like those of humans, show up as white on an X-ray screen (below). Such images can be used to study the bone structure and development of living fishes, and also to investigate fish diseases.

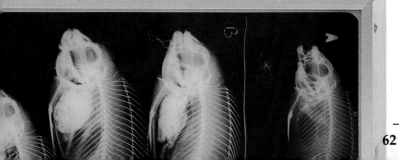

IN GOOD SPIRITS
Fish specimens are "fixed" in formaldehyde to stop the tissues from decaying. They are then stored permanently in alcohol. Colors tend to fade, but every detail of the internal structure is preserved.

Tight-fitting lid to prevent evaporation of alcohol

Suitably shaped specimen jar

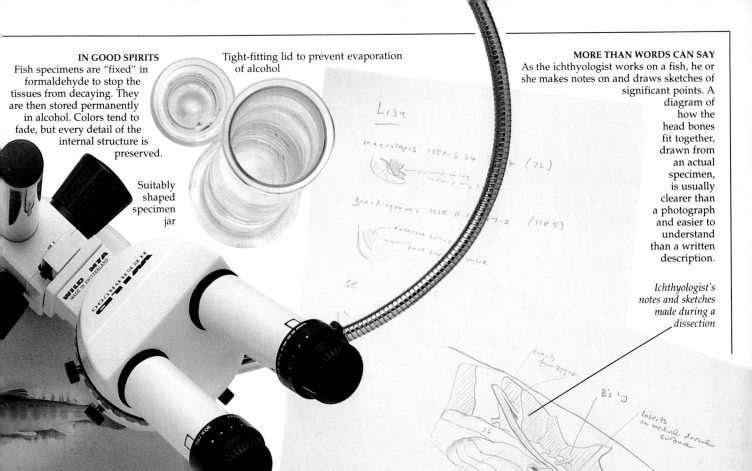

MORE THAN WORDS CAN SAY
As the ichthyologist works on a fish, he or she makes notes on and draws sketches of significant points. A diagram of how the head bones fit together, drawn from an actual specimen, is usually clearer than a photograph and easier to understand than a written description.

Ichthyologist's notes and sketches made during a dissection

UNDER THE MICROSCOPE
Various types of microscopes are used to look at the fish in greater and greater detail. A binocular or dissecting microscope (above) reveals parts that are slightly too small for the naked eye, at a magnification of about 10-50 times. The scanning electron microscope, or SEM (right), shows surface details at over 10,000 times life-size.

Two eyepieces of binocular microscope give 3D "depth" to the view, unlike a single-eyepiece microscope

Modern technology: a scientist working on a scanning electron microscope (SEM)

Dial calipers

MEASURING FISHES
The dial calipers are one of several accurate instruments for measuring the size of fish features, from the height of the tail to the diameter of an eye or a tiny scale. Such information is recorded in tables and charts (right).

RAW DATA
Sets of basic measurements of fishes – color, scale type, etc. – are analyzed, often by computer, and compiled into a "database summary" for that particular fish or group of fishes. This data can be used to tell species apart, or the number of fishes there are in a species. The information may then be published in scientific journals where other experts can read them.

Raw data for computers

Did you know?

FASCINATING FACTS

Koi fish often outlive their original owners and are handed down to the next generation. Although the average lifespan of a koi is between 40 and 60 years old, one koi in Japan was reported to be 230 years old!

Who are you calling big mouth? The goosefish has an enormous, toothy mouth. This fish is capable of eating huge amounts of almost anything, from sea turtles to the birds that gave it its nickname. A goosefish can even swallow other fish that are equal to its own weight.

Koi fish are so tame you can feed them by hand.

Don't put your money on a seahorse. They are among the slowest swimmers in the sea.

Is that fish a gramma or a grandpa? The gramma fish can change sex at will. If there are no males around to mate with, the female gramma changes into a male.

Seahorses

You've probably heard of electric eels, but there are also several kinds of electric fish. A type of ray, a catfish, and the stargazer all use electricity to paralyze or kill their prey or repel advancing enemies.

Puffer fish can puff themselves up with air and water when a predator approaches, but what they really like to fill up on is food! It is said that the fish will eat and continue to eat until it is almost unconscious.

Dorsal (tail) fin used in swimming

The batfish plays dead when danger is near. It floats motionless on its side when alarmed, resembling a dead leaf floating on the surface of the water.

You'll know when you've spotted the reef-dweller from Australia called the pineapple fish. Its golden yellow scales edged in black resemble the pattern on the tropical fruit's exterior.

Sea anemone's poison stinger

Coral reef

Fish clustering near tentacles for protection

A fish fry is not just the name of something to enjoy with cole slaw, hush puppies, and ttartar sauce. It is the rather unfortunate name for a baby fish!

Flashlight fish never need to wonder who turned off the lights. On the darkest of nights, these fish give off a strange green glow to help them see. The light is generated by bacteria living in special pouches on the fish's jaws.

The candiru is a tiny little fish with a nearly transparent body that makes it very difficult to see—not that you would want to. This scary fish from the Amazon and Orinoco Rivers of South America has a vampire's thirst for blood, human or animal.

Anableps (four-eye fish) can see above and below water at the same time—very handy for finding food and for avoiding becoming food.

How old is a fish? One way to age a fish is by its scales. Like trees, they have growth rings called circuli that can reveal the fish's age.

The rabbitfish gets its name from three bunny-like features: its slight overbite, exposing buck teeth, its large, dark eyes, and its tendency to constantly nibble like a rabbit.

Rains of fish have been documented in several cases. If winds are strong enough, mini-tornadoes form. When these pass over water they pick up fish and carry them into the clouds. When the clouds later open and rain begins to fall, so do the fish. These showers are not as uncommon as you might think, and they have been written about for thousands of years. Roman writer Pliny the Younger described a fishy rain in the 1st century C.E.

Coral's hard skeleton is secreted by marine creatures.

QUESTIONS AND ANSWERS

Whale shark

Piranha

How fast can fish swim?

Billed fish like the marlin and the swordfish are speedy indeed, but the sailfish is the fastest thing on fins. This fish has been measured at speeds of up to 68 mph (109 kph). That's faster than a cheetah!

How far can a fish swim?

Salmon have been known to travel 2,000 miles (3,218 km) to reach the exact stream they were hatched in at spawning time.

Which fish lays the most eggs?

The ocean sunfish has a round, flat body that looks a little like a huge lima bean. This fish lays an incredible 30 million eggs in one spawning, making it by far the most fertile in the fish world.

Which is the largest predator fish?

With a conveyer-belt like set of 3,000 teeth, the great white shark is the ocean's largest and most feared predator. These 20-foot-(6-m-) long beasts prowl the world's subtropical waters. Like most animals, great white sharks would rather avoid you than attack you.

Which is the most ferocious predatory fish in fresh water?

That would have to be the legendary South African piranha. This river fish has a mouthful of sharp triangular teeth that help it chop through its prey. Although reports of piranha attacks on humans have been exaggerated, it's best not to find out firsthand if their deadly reputation is a deserved one.

Do fish hear?

Yes, but hearing abilities vary by species. A fish hears as sensory chambers in its inner ear detect differences in sound vibrations. In some fish, the swim bladder plays a role in transmitting these vibrations. If you tap on the glass of an aquarium, a fish will "hear" it as pressure against the side of its body.

Mouthful of teeth

White underside helps shark "disappear" when it is near the lighter surface.

Triangular fins

Great white shark

What is the largest fish?

The enormous whale shark has been recorded at 41.5 ft (12.65 m) long. Its mouth alone is a staggering 4 ft (1.2 m) wide! This supersized fish, found in the warm parts of the Atlantic, Pacific, and Indian Oceans, is a filter feeder. It eats the vast numbers of plankton that pass through its toothy grin as it moves along.

Which is the oldest kind of fish?

The lampreys and hagfishes are the most primitive fish still living today. These odd-looking bottom-dwellers have rounded, sucking mouths. We know that jawless fish are older because the fossil record shows that later fish evolved biting jaws.

Do fish sleep?

That depends on how you define sleep. Fish do not share the brain wave changes of human sleep, but they do have sleep-like periods of reduced metabolism, lowered response to stimuli, and slowed physical activity.

Do flying fish really fly?

No. They jump out of the water and glide, as their lower tail lobe works rather like an outboard motor to help them move. "Flights" of more than 300 ft (91.44 m) have been known, but a typical glide distance is much shorter.

What is the smallest freshwater fish?

The dwarf goby lives in the Indo-Pacific Ocean, but you might not notice. This little fish is only about 0.3 inches (0.0076 m) long. The smallest freshwater fish, the pygmy goby, is even tinier. It only grows to about 0.28 inches (0.0071 m) long and weighs under an ounce!

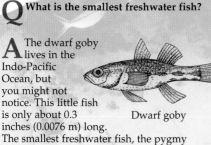
Dwarf goby

Freaky fish stories

Fish have been around for some 500 million years, but they're still making news. Here are the true tales of some extremely odd fish.

In 2002, a strange "Frankenfish" crawled from a murky Maryland pond. These snakeheads, able to breathe air and waddle on land for days, caused a sensation as they gobbled up frogs, birds—even small mammals.

A man leaning over an aquarium exhibit wall to retrieve his son's cap in 2004 accidentally dropped his cell phone into the water. A huge catfish promptly ate it in one bite. The man's attempts to call his own cell phone number to see which fish vibrated did not work.

In a scene from the hit 2003 movie *Finding Nemo*, a fish is flushed down the toilet to return to the sea. After parents reported cases of hundreds of children setting their fish "free" in the same way, the film studio had to launch "Don't Flush the Fish" campaigns across the globe.

Would you like a beverage with your meal? In 2004, a Norwegian fisherman was stunned when a codfish he hauled in with his daily catch contained an intact, unopened cola can. The can had even kept its bright red color.

Fish tales

FISH HAVE BEEN AROUND for nearly 500 million years, so it's no surprise that these fascinating finned creatures are among the most important symbols in the world's myths and legends. There are tales of horrible monsters and heroic gods, wily tricksters and outright hoaxers, the lure of a mermaid and the lie about the one that got away. Here's the place to dip into a few of these fishy fables.

Triton's conch shells

Gods and heroes

Throughout world mythology, gods and heroes appear in the guise of fish. Sometimes, the gods are half human and half fish. In other tales, gods change into fish for protection. Fish are often associated with life and creation because fish live in the waters from which all life springs.

WHAT A CATCH!
New Zealand legend tells of a hero named Maui who cast a magic fish hook. When the hook snagged something, Maui and his brothers pulled with all their might—and raised the North Island of New Zealand right out of the waters.

FLOOD WARNING
The supreme Hindu god, Vishnu, appeared to humans in ten *avatars* (incarnations) to provide help. In his first avatar, he took the form of a fish to warn humankind of a terrible flood.

THE ONES THAT GOT AWAY
In Roman mythology, a pair of gods called Venus and Cupid were out for a riverside stroll when they encountered Typhon, a horrible giant. Terrified, they jumped into the river and took the form of fish. The other gods lifted the fish into the sky to form the constellation Pisces.

SCHOOL OF FISH
The Mesopotamian god Oannes brought wisdom to humans. With a man's head on a fish's body, he rose from the sea bed each day to teach science and art.

Triton statue and fountain

TRITON CALLING
This mythological creature, half man and half fish, is the son of Poseidon, the ruler of the seas. As seen in this statue, Triton is often depicted with a conch shell. He can raise or lower the ocean waves with a single call from his shell.

Fish and Christianity

The fish is one of the earliest symbols in the religion of Christianity, representing both Jesus Christ and his believers. Fish tales appear in both the Old and New Testaments of the Bible, and Jesus is sometimes referred to as a "fisher of men."

LOAVES AND FISHES
In one of the miracles of the Christian Bible, Jesus feeds a crowd of five thousand with just five loaves of bread and two fish.

JONAH AND THE BIG FISH
In the Bible, a man named Jonah refuses to follow God's instructions, and tries to escape God's wrath by taking a long sailing trip. At sea, mighty winds and waves sent by God cause the ship to wreck, and Jonah is gobbled up by a gigantic fish. He stays inside the fish for three days and three nights until Jonah asks God for a second chance and the fish coughs him up alive.

HOLY FISH
The bishop fish is a European sea monster with the shaved head of a monk and the body of an fish. In one tale, Catholic bishops meet a captured bishop fish. The monster makes a gesture indicating its wish to be set free. They let it go, and the fish make the sign of the cross before slipping back into the sea.

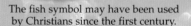

The fish symbol may have been used by Christians since the first century.

CHRISTIAN SYMBOL
In Christianity, the fish is a symbol for Christ. This may be because in Greek, the first letters of the words, Jesus Christ Son of God spell *Ichthus*, or fish.

MORE HOLY FISH
Celtic legends tell of magical fish that live in pairs in wells near churches. They nibble the hazelnuts that fall from the trees above the well. This diet gives them special properties, including the ability to speak. Harming a holy fish in any way would invite divine retribution.

Tile mosaic representing the miracle of the loaves and fishes

Monsters of the deep

Although sea creatures and other water dwellers in mythology were usually benign, there were many fabled fish who were downright monstrous.

Engraving of fishy sea monsters lurking in the waters

HIPPOCAMP
This creature is a sea animal from Greek mythology. Its head resembles a horse, and its hind parts a fish. Poseidon, the god of the sea, hitches the Hippocamp to his chariot to pull it across the waves.

CALL OF THE MERMAID
Mermaids and sirens appear in the mythology of many peoples. The mermaid has the body of a woman and the curving tail of a fish. Sometimes she carries a mirror, to represent truth. A siren may also appear in the half-female, half-fish guise. Her voice has the power to lure men to their deaths.

Mermaid statue in Copenhagen, Denmark

NIXES
Norse folklore tells tales of nixes, water spirits that try to lure people into the water to drown. A nix may appear as a fish or a human. When nixes are in human form, there is said to be one way to spot them: The hems of their clothes are wet.

POISON ARROWS
Throughout world mythology fish are usually portrayed as benevolent creatures. But in the legends of the islands of Pacific Islands, there are some pretty fishy characters. The adaro, for example, is a nasty sea-spirit who is half human, half fish. This creature has gills behind his ears, fins for feet, and a pike on his head like a swordfish. He rides across the waves on rainbows, killing people by shooting poisonous fish at them just like arrows.

SHARK ATTACK!
The mythology of the Hawaiian Islands features shark gods as well as people who can change from human to shark. In many tales, these monsters take human forms, then rush up to people on the beach to warn them to stay out of the shark-infested waters. The beachgoers laugh off the warnings and dive in, only to be chomped by the same creature in shark form.

SCARY SEA CREATURES
During the Age of Exploration, little was known about what lurked in the waters. Many a sailor feared sailing off the edge of the world, but they were also scared of being gobbled by a gigantic sea monster after a shipwreck. This engraving served as a catalog of various sea beasts to watch out for. In truth, sailors probably mistook more unusual-looking fish (like the long eel-like oarfish) for monsters.

SIDESHOW HOAX
In 1842, legendary showman P.T. Barnum exhibited the remains of a Feejee (now Fiji) Mermaid. He paid a fortune for the skeleton, but soon earned that money back as people crowded into his museum to see this strange and mysterious artifact. The mermaid, however, was a hoax; it was made from the preserved body of a skate, a type of flatfish.

Fish as symbols

From the signs of the zodiac to a sign of wealth, fish appear as symbols in the lore of many lands. Fish are often associated with fertility, and many cultures consider fish to be a source of wisdom and power. In many cultures, fish symbolize the cycle of death and rebirth.

THE SIGN OF THE FISH
The idea that the movement of the Sun, the Moon, and other heavenly bodies affects our lives goes back thousands of years. As early as 3000 B.C.E., ancient Mesopotamian scholars recorded the signs of the zodiac we know today. Each of the 12 star signs shows one-twelfth of the heavens at the time of a person's birth. The pair of fishes, called Pisces, represents the star constellation of the same name.

Woodcut of Pisces symbol

GOOD LUCK FISH
In Japan, the tai fish (a sea bream) is considered a symbol of good luck: no important celebration is complete without one. In the spring these fish take on a reddish color. Because red is also a lucky color, tai are especially prized at that time.

FISHING FOR WEALTH
For thousands of years, the carp has been a symbol of wealth and power in China. People wishing for success in life are encouraged to display an image of a golden carp in their homes in the Chinese practice of Feng Shui.

SYMBOLIC SALMON
An important symbol among Native American tribes who live in the Pacific Northwest is the salmon. This fish is a staple food of the region, but it holds strong symbolic power as well. Because it swims so determinedly upstream to find its birthplace, it represents courage and perseverance.

Native American salmon woodcarving

Find out more

THERE'S A WHOLE WORLD of fish to discover—here's how to dive in! An excellent place to begin is at an aquarium; here you'll find exhibits featuring fish from the world's 20,000 species. A visit to a natural history museum will show you everything you need to know about both prehistoric and modern fish through fossils, skeletons, and specimens. You could also visit an aquatic theme park. Learning how to snorkel or scuba-dive will bring you eye-to-eye with an oceanful of fish, or you might want to purchase an aquarium to create your own small-scale aquatic community.

A TUNNEL OF FISH

Splashing down into an aquarium is one of the best ways to get under the waves without getting wet! The only thing separating you from an amazing array of fish is a thick glass wall. Check out the box on the opposite page for some excellent aquaria across the country. Many aquaria feature freshwater fish, marine fish, and a host of other sea creatures to help you understand and explore fish habitats. The Audubon Aquarium of the Americas in New Orleans features a crystal clear tunnel (left) that gives aquarium visitors the experience of being surrounded on three sides by water—and fish. From time to time, an aquarium employee dons scuba gear to feed and care for the fish and carry out maintenance tasks.

Large mouth gulps plenty of plankton

UP THE RIVER WITH A PADDLE

Some aquaria focus on the freshwater fish of the Earth's lakes and rivers. Learn about this unusual paddlefish in the Tennessee Aquarium's Mississippi River exhibit. Its paddle is covered in taste buds and nerve endings that help it find plankton as it cruises the river.

USEFUL WEB SITES

- Explore the ocean realm with the National Oceanic and Atmospheric Administration: **http://oceanexplorer.noaa.gov**
- The home site of the Monterey Bay Aquarium Research Institute: **www.mbari.org**
- The official site of the New England Aquarium is a one-stop place for information: **www.neaq.org**
- Home page of the South Carolina Aquarium and an excellent source for info on freshwater habitats: **www.scaquarium.org**
- The Woods Hole Oceanographic Institute is dedicated to the study of marine science: **www.whoi.edu**

HANDS-ON LEARNING

Many aquaria and aquatic parks feature tidepool exhibits and small tanks that allow you to hold and touch fish specimens. These young visitors to the Monterey Bay Aquarium in California are reaching out to touch swimming bat rays.

FISH ON FILM

Recent movies such as *Shark Tale* bring the undersea world to life through amazing computer animation. Although their stories are strictly fantasy, these movies serve to illustrate the fascination which fish and other marine life continue to hold for those of us who live on land.

A WINDOW TO THE WORLD OF FISH

A fish tank is a great way to observe a habitat on a much smaller scale. You can purchase starter sets that contain everything you need to begin at most pet stores. Remember that fish are living creatures and it is your responsibility to provide them with an environment in which they can thrive.

Rocks and plants create a lifelike habitat.

DOWN TIME

With the silvery surface of the sea above you and thousands of fish swimming by all around you, scuba diving is as close as you are ever going to get to being a fish yourself! Divers usually need to complete a 20-hour certification course run by one of the sport's major organizations (check the Internet or your phone book). Or, if you are lucky enough to visit a tropical resort, you can complete a resort course that allows you to dive with an instructor.

Fish have gills, but you'll need a tank.

Places to Visit

MONTEREY BAY AQUARIUM, MONTEREY, CA
This award-winning aquarium with more than 200 exhibits recently celebrated its 20th anniversary. It is steps from the Pacific Ocean.

SHEDD AQUARIUM, CHICAGO, IL
The largest indoor aquarium in the world, the Shedd features 8,000 different marine animals.

NATIONAL AQUARIUM, WASHINGTON, D.C.
America's oldest aquarium, this national treasure features more than 80 exhibits with 2,000 freshwater and marine species.

NEW ENGLAND AQUARIUM, BOSTON, MA
Located on Boston's thriving waterfront, this aquarium aims to provide a complete underwater experience for its visitors.

VANCOUVER AQUARIUM, VANCOUVER, CANADA
Canada's largest aquarium features 8,000 animals and an Arctic Habitat exhibit.

TENNESEE AQUARIUM, CHATTANOOGA, TN
See more than 300 species of fish with a special focus on the freshwater fish of the Southeast.

NEW YORK AQUARIUM BROOKLYN, NY
Where the city meets the sea, you will encounter more than 8,000 species in this Coney Island institution.

AUDUBON AQUARIUM OF THE AMERICAS NEW ORLEANS, LA
Take an amazing trip through an aquatic tunnel 30 feet (9 m) long. You'll be surrounded by 132,000 gallons of water—and a lot of fish.

Glossary

Shark's dorsal fin helps steer and stop

ACANTHODIAN An ancient shark-like fish with spiny fins

AMPHIBIAN Any vertebrate, including frogs, toads, newts, and salamanders, that usually begins life in the water as a tadpole with gills and later develops lungs

ANADROMOUS Any fish that go up rivers to spawn

AQUATIC Growing or living, or taking place, in or upon water

BARBEL One of the fleshy, touch-sensitive whiskers on certain fish, like catfish; also called a barb

BRACKISH Somewhat salty water, like the water found in a marsh

BREACHING When a whale leaps clear out of the ocean water

BUOYANCY The tendency or ability to float or rise in liquid or air

CAMOUFLAGE Any of the ways by which an animal conceals itself, for example, from a predator

CARTILAGINOUS Having a skeleton made up mostly of cartilage (tough, elastic tissue)

CAUDAL At or near the tail

Caudal fin

CHROMATOPHORE A finely branched skin pigment (coloration) cell

CICHLIDS Any of a family of tropical and subtropical freshwater fish that are similar to sunfish

COCOON Any protective cover in which an immature animal shelters itself during one of its life stages

COELACANTH A primitive fish (dating back some 400 million years) once known only in fossil form; living specimens first found in South Africa in 1938

CORAL The hard, rock-like skeleton secreted by certain marine polyps and deposited in extensive masses

CORAL REEF A ridge built mostly of coral in shallow, tropical seas

COUNTERSHADING Animal coloring with a darker back and paler belly

CRUSTACEANS Any of a class of arthropods, including shrimps, crabs, barnacles, and lobsters, that usually live in water and breathe through gills; they have hard outer shells

CTENOID Having an edge with projections like the teeth of a comb

CYCLOID Having fish scales that are rounded in form with smooth edges

DENTICLE A small tooth, or a tooth-like projection

DERMIS The layer of skin just below the epidermis, which is the outermost layer

DORSAL Of or on the back

EEL Any of a large variety of fish with long, slippery snake-like bodies and no pelvic fin

EGG CASE Protective sac where an embryo grows

ELASMOBRANCH A class of fishes with cartilaginous skeletons, placoid scales, and lack of air bladders

EMBRYO An animal in the earliest stages of its development

EXOSKELETON Any hard, secreted external supporting structure, like an oyster's shell

FERTILIZE In biology, to impregnate or pollinate and make fruitful

FIN Any of several wing-like, membranous bodies on a fish, used in swimming, turning, and balancing

FISH Any of a large group of cold-blooded vertebrate animals living in water; fish have permanent gills for breathing, fins, and usually scales

GANOID Of a group of primitive fishes covered by rows of hard, glossy enameled scales or plates

GILL The breathing organ for most animals that live in water

HALFBEAK Any of the long-bodied, small tropical sea fishes with extended lower jaws and short upper jaws

Shark in profile

HYPEROSTEOSIS A thickening or abnormal increase in the formation of bone

ICHTHYOLOGY The branch of zoology dealing with fishes, their structure, classification, and life history

LARVAL Of the immature form of an animal before it reaches adulthood

LATERAL LINE A row of sensory organs along each side of the head and body of a fish, probably used to detect currents, vibrations, and pressure changes

LEPIDOTRICHS On a fish, the long and thin fin rays that support all dorsal and anal fins

LOBES A rounded, projecting part of the body

MAMMAL Any of a large class of warm-blooded, usually hairy vertebrates whose babies are fed with mother's milk

MEDIAN FINS In a fish, the unpaired fins: dorsal, anal or ventral, and caudal

MEMBRANE A thin, soft, pliable sheet of animal tissue, serving as a covering or lining for an organ or for a body part

METAMORPHOSIS In biology, a change in form, structure, or function as a result of development

Egg case

MERMAID'S PURSE Nickname for the hard, dried-out egg cases of certain fish that wash up on the beach

MILT The reproductive glands of male fishes, and the cells and fluid they contain

MOUTHBROODERS Any of the fishes that care for their eggs and young in their mouth and throat

MUCUS The thick, slimy substance secreted by mucous membranes that moistens and protects them

MYOTOME The body-wall muscles in a single segment.

OPERCULUM The bony covering protecting the gills of fishes

OVIPAROUS Producing eggs which hatch after leaving the body of the female

PAIRED FINS On a fish, a set of fins with one on each side of the body; pectoral and pelvic fins, for example

PARASITE A plant or animal that lives on or in an organism from a different species; derives protection or food from its host without benefiting the host

PECTORAL FIN One of a pair of fins just behind the head of a fish

PELVIC FIN One of a pair of fins at the pelvic girdle of a fish

PHARYNGEAL Of or found in the throat

PHARYNX The cavity leading from the mouth and nasal passages to the larynx and esophagus

PITCH Up or down movement of a fish

Prehensile tail

Yellow seahorse

PLACOID Of or having horny scales with a dentine base and a tooth-like spine

PREDATOR One who captures and feeds on other animals

PREHENSILE Adapted for grasping by wrapping or folding around something

PROPULSION Something that pushes or drives an object forward

REPTILE Any of a class of cold-blooded vertebrates having lungs, a bony skeleton, a body covered with scales or plates, and a heart with two chambers

ROE Fish eggs, especially when massed together in the ovarian membrane

ROLL To rotate on its own axis; for example, when a fish swims

SCALES Any of the thin, flat, overlapping plates forming the outer protective covering of a fish

SCHOOL A large number of fish of the same kind swimming together

SCUTES Any external bony or horny plate

SEAHORSE Any of the marine fishes with a slender tail, a plated body, and a head somewhat like a horse

SEINE NET A fishing net with floats along the top edge and weights on the bottom

SHELLFISH Any aquatic animal with a shell; for example, a lobster or clam

Tubelike mouth

SPAWNING Producing or depositing eggs or young

SPECIES In biology, a classification of plants or animals; members of a class have a high degree of similarity, can usually breed only among themselves, and show differences from other species

SPECIMEN In science, an example of a particular species prepared or used for study of the whole species

SPINE A sharp, stiff projection on the body of certain animals; for example, on a ray of a fish's fin

SPIRACLE A circular opening for air or respiratory water

SPIRAL VALVE The lower portion of the digestive tract

STREAMLINING A way of contouring that offers the least resistance when moving through water or air

SWIM BLADDER A gas-filled sac in the dorsal portion of the body cavity in most fish which gives the body buoyancy

TARPON A large, silvery game fish with large scales

TELOSTS Any of the large subclass of bony fish with a symmetrical tail fin and an air bladder

Scales

TENTACLES Any of a variety of long, slender growths around the head and mouth used for sensing, moving, etc.

TETRODOTOXIN An extremely poisonous substance found in puffer fish

TOXIN Any of the various poisons secreted by certain animals

TRANSPARENT Capable of being seen through; neither opaque nor transluscent

TRANSVERSE LINE A crosswise line; on a fish, the lateral line runs the length of the body while the transverse line runs from back to belly

TRAWL A large, bag-like net dragged along behind a fishing boat

TROPICAL Of the region on Earth between the Tropic of Cancer and the Tropic of Capricorn

VENOMOUS Containing or full of venom; poisonous

VERTEBRAL COLUMN The spinal column or backbone

VIVIPAROUS Bearing live young (as most mammals do) instead of laying eggs

WHALE Any of a large, warm-blooded fish-like mammals that breathe air, bear live young, and have front flippers and a flat, horizontal tail

YAW To swing on the vertical axis; for example, as a fish swims

Ray's fins contain visible spines

Female thornback ray

YOLK SAC In zoology, the sac-like membrane containing yolk, the protein and fat contents that nourish an embryo

Index

A

acanthodian 12
actinopterygians 9
agnathans 9
amphibians 6, 12
angel fishes 15, 16, 20
anglerfish 20, 21
arawana 37, 44
archerfishes 36
armor 10, 15, 30, 31
Atlantic blue tang 17

B

barracuda 35
basking shark 10, 61
beluga sturgeon 42
bichir 9
bitterling 43
black goby 40
blenny 32
blue-ringed angelfish 17
blue shark 19, 30, 58
body shape 8, 20, 21
bonytongue 45
bottle-nosed dolphin 7
bowfin 9, 41
bream 34
breeding 23, 40, 41, 42, 52
brills 35
bullhead sharks 42, 54
burrfishes 39
butterflyfish 16, 17, 30, 36

C

california blind gobies 24
camouflage 6, 10, 16, 17,
    20, 21, 22, 23, 26, 27, 35,
    38, 46, 56, 58
carpet sharks
    (wobbegong) 19, 58
carps 6, 8, 9, 15
cartilaginous fishes 6, 8, 9,
    10, 35, 54, 56, 59
cascadura 10
catfishes 10, 15, 19, 28, 30,
    31, 32, 38, 48, 54
catshark 59

Cephalaspis 12, 13
chimaeras 9, 20, 42, 54
chondrichthians 9
cichlids 17, 19, 44, 45
Cladoselache 58
cleaners 46, 47
climbing perches 32,
clingfish 21
clown loach 16
clown triggerfish 17
clownfishes 46, 47
cod 10, 11, 20, 27, 42
coelacanth 9, 12, 13, 14
color 16, 17, 18, 19, 20, 22,
    26, 40
conger eel 48, 49
coral reefs 6, 16, 17, 18, 31,
    35, 36, 38, 50
countershading 18, 19, 28,
    52, 59
cowfish 21
crossopterygians 9
crucian carp 18
crustaceans 7, 35
Cuban hock 17

D

dabs 25, 26
dace 52
damselfishes 46
Dapedium 13
Darwin, Charles 62
dealfish 25, 48
defense 16, 17, 38, 54, 55,
    56
dipnoi 9
discus fish 45
dogfishes 28, 43, 54, 60
dragonet 17, 41
drumfishes 19,
dwarf gourami 41
dwarf pygmy goby 6

E

eagle rays 54
eels 28, 29, 48, 49
elasmobranchs 9
electric eel 48, 49
electric organs 57
elephant-trunk fish 20, 34
Eurypholis 13
Eusthenopteron 13
eyesight 7, 52, 58

F

feeding methods 34, 35
    36, 37
filefish 51
fin rays 6, 11, 17, 25, 27,
    30, 31 32
flag cichlid 19
flatfishes 24, 25 , 26, 27,
    54, 56, 57
flounders 25, 27
flying fishes 31
forceps fish 16, 35
fossils 9, 12, 13, 56, 61
frilled shark 58

G

garden eels 51
garfish 11, 14
gars 9, 11, 13, 14, 20
giant gar 13
glass catfish 10
goby 50, 51
goldfish 18
great white shark 59, 61
grouper 47
gulpers 48
gurnard 30, 32

H

hagfishes 8, 9, 12
halfbeak 35
halibuts 25
hammerhead shark 59
harlequin frog fish 21
hatchetfish 21
Heliobatis 13
herring 10, 52, 58
high-hat drum 19
holocephalans 9, 20
holosteans 9, 11, 13, 41

I J K

Indian snakehead 9
insects 36, 37
internal organs 8, 10, 25, 27
Ischnacanthus 12
jawless fishes 8, 9, 12
John Dory 20, 34
knifefishes 21, 48

L

lampreys 9, 12, 34
larval fish 24, 25
lateral line 7, 8, 15, 28, 52
Lear, Edward 32
leather carp 15
leatherjacket 35
lesser spotted dogfish 29,
    60
lesser weever 55
lionfishes 31, 54, 55
loaches 16
lobe-finned fishes 9, 13
long-nosed gar 20
loosejaw 18
luminous organs 18, 39
lungfishes 8, 9 13, 32, 45

M

mackerel 8, 10, 19, 58
mako shark 61
mandarin fish 17
mangrove swamps 32, 36
manta ray 57
megrim 25
mermaid's purse 43
metamorphosis 24, 25, 26
miller's thumb 42
mirror carp 15
mollusks 7, 35
morays 48, 50
mouthbooders 44
mucus 6, 14, 47
mudskippers 32, 33
mussels 34, 43

O

oarfish 48
octopus 49
operculum 7, 8, 59
osteichthyans 9
osteotracans 12
overfishing 52, 62

P

pacu 34
paddlefish 9
Palaeoniscus 12

panther grouper 19
parasites 6, 46, 47
parental care 44, 45
parrotfishes 31, 35
perch 8, 9
pike 11
pike eels 48
pilchard 58
pilot fish 46
pipefish 16, 22, 23 44
piranha 35
piracuru (arapaima) 9
plaice 25, 26, 27
plankton 34, 35, 49, 52, 57
porcupine fish 15, 21, 34,
    38, 39, 62
Port Jackson shark 43, 60
Portuguese man-of-war
    46
Procarcharodon 61
Pteraclis 31
pufferfishes 38, 39, 54
pygmy devil 57

R

rabbitfishes 9, 20, 54
rainbow trout 18
ratfish 9, 20
ray-finned fishes 9, 12
rays 9, 12, 13, 14, 29, 35,
    42, 43, 54, 56, 57
red mullet 19
remora 30
reptiles 6, 8, 12
ribbon eel 48
ribbonfish 25
royal gramma 16
rudd 18

S

sailfish 11, 30
salmon 7, 42
sand eels 56
sarcopterygians 9
sawfish 35, 56
scaled dragonfish 38
Schmidt, Johannes 49
Scleropages 44
scorpionfish 46, 54, 55
sea anemones 46, 47
sea catfish 31, 44
sea lions 60
sea stickleback 40

seadragon 23
seahorse 22, 23, 44
shepherdfishes 46
shrimpfishes 21
skates 9, 42, 56
sole 24, 25, 27
spadefish 11
spiny boxfish 21
sprats 56
squid 60
stargazer 54
Stichocentrus 13
stingrays 23, 54, 59
stonefishes 35, 54, 55
sturgeon 9, 10, 14, 30
surgeonfishes 17, 38
swim bladder 8, 9 23
swordfish 34, 35

T

tail "mouth" 17
tarpon 15
tassel-finned fishes 9
teleosts 9, 10, 13
tench 18
thornback ray 56, 57
three-spined stickleback
    40, 41, 43
thresher shark 58, 61
tiger shark 60
toadfishes 54
topknots 25
torpedo 57
triggerfish 31, 35, 38, 51
tripod fish 33
trout 36
trumpetfish 34
trunkfish 10, 11
tuna 9, 30, 52
turbots 25, 27, 42

W Y

weevers 54
whale shark 6, 10, 34, 58,
    61
whales 6, 28
wrasses 16, 17, 47, 50, 51
yellowtail snappers 53

Acknowledgments

The publisher would like to thank:
Geoff Potts, Fred Frettsome, and Vicky Irlam at the Marine Biological Association, Plymoth; Rick Elliot, and the staff at Waterlife Research Industries Ltd; Neil Fletcher, Simon Newnes & Partners, Billingsgate, London; Richard Davies of OSF for photography on pp. 28-29, 23-33; Bari Howell at MAFF, Conwy for supplying eggs and hatchings on pp. 24-25; Barney Kindersley; Lester Cheeseman and Jane Coney for additional design work; Jane Parker for the index.

Picture Credits
(t =top, b=bottom, m=middle, l=left, r=right)

Ardea: 37mr, 58tl
Biofotos/Heather Angel: 32tl
Anthony Blake / Roux Bros: 42tl

Bruce Coleman Ltd / Kim Taylor: 43tl
Philip Dowell: 18tl, 18ml, 18br
Mary Evans Picture Library: 29br, 55tl
Robert Harding Picture Library: 29br, 55tl
Dave King: 27mr
Kobal Collection: 59bl
Frank Lane Picture Agency/Stevie McCutcheon" 28tr
David Morbey/ Natural History Museum: 63m
A. Van den Nieuwenhuizen: 28b
Planet Earth Pictures: 44tr, 44ml, 53tl, 60bl; James King: 52bl; John & Gillian Lythgoe: 49tr;
Jane McKinnon: 23tm, Paulo Oliveria: 45tl; Peter Scoones: 11br, 51tr; Bill Wood: 47t; Gary Summons/Natural History Museum: 62t
Survival Anglia/Alan Root: 33tr
Frank Spooner Pictures: 54m, 54bm, 54bl
Zefa/J.Schupe: 7tr

AKG-Images: 67tr; Hilbich 66tr

Audubon Nature Institute: David Bull 68ml

Corbis: DreamWorks Animation/ Bureau L.A.Collections 69t; Amos Nachoum 65tl; Jeffrey L. Rotman 69b; Vince Streano 64tm

Dorling Kindersley: 65tr, 67bl; Paul Bricknell 69m; Jane Burton71ml; Demetrio Carrasco 67tl; Alistair Duncan 66bl; Ken Findlay 64b; Frank Greenaway 65 br, 70t; Dave King 71tr; Rodney Shackell 65bl; Kim Taylor 70br; Eric Thomas 66br, Jerry Young 64ml, 70l, 71b

Monterey Bay Aquarium Foundation: Randy Wilder 68br

Seattle Art Museum, Gift of John H. Hauberg: 67br

Tennessee Aquarium: Richard T. Bryant 68bl; Todd Stanley 68tl

Front cover: B: Norbert Wu/Minden/ FLPA

Illustrations by: John Woodcock

Picture Research by: Kathy Lockley

All other images © Dorling Kindersley

For more information see:
www.dkimages.com